Resource and Environmental Sciences Series

General Editors:
Sir Alan Cottrell, FRS
Professor T. R. E. Southwood, FRS

Environmental Economics:

An Introduction for students of the Resource and
Environmental Sciences

Alan Cottrell, ScD, FRS

Jesus College, Cambridge

A HALSTED PRESS BOOK

JOHN WILEY & SONS
New York

© Alan Cottrell 1978

First published 1978 by
Edward Arnold (Publishers) Ltd
London

Published in the U.S.A.
by Halsted Press, a Division
of John Wiley & Sons, Inc.
New York

Library of Congress Cataloging in Publication Data

Cottrell, Alan Howard.
    Environmental economics.

    (Resource and environmental sciences series)
    "A Halsted Press book."
    Includes index.
    1.   Environmental policy. 2. Economics.
3. Conservation of natural resources. 4. Human
ecology. I. Title. II. Series.
HC79.E5C67   1977   301.31   77-27582
ISBN 0-470-99395-2

Printed in Great Britain

Preface

Many students of the biological and physical sciences have become keenly interested in problems of the earth's natural resources and the quality of its environment. They may however be less familiar with the concepts of the major discipline already in the field — the science of economics, which studies man's use of scarce resources. This booklet, in no sense an economics text, has been written to give such students some feeling for the economic dimension of their subject; for what determines the costs and prices of such basic human requirements as energy, food, minerals, and a clean environment; for the factors that underlie the present and future capacity of the earth to support mankind; and for the trade-offs between economic growth, population growth, consumption of resources and environmental protection. There are strong reasons for believing that the world is about to enter an Age of Scarcity; the new science of Environmental Economics may help to guide us through this dangerous period.

Cambridge
1977   A.H.C.

Contents

1 Earth, Air, Fire and Water

Scarce Resources

The best things in life are free. So the saying goes. Certainly, so far as natural resources are concerned, Man has free run of this planet, with its earth, air, fire and water, which the classical Greeks saw as the elements of everything. But what is given to Man is not necessarily given freely in abundance to everyone, for, with so many people wanting so much in the world today, many resources are scarce. The only one still obviously free for all is air, but even here problems of air pollution set limits to the freedom of the air. Feelings ran so high on this subject, in 14th century London, that a man was hanged for burning smoky coal.

Almost as free as air is fresh water, at least in rain-washed countries. The 'water rate', which a householder generally pays in such a country, is essentially a payment for the service of having pure water piped into his home; the restrictions then placed on how much he can use are usually minimal. Sea water is free for all but not worth piping inland because its saltiness ruins its *utility* for most purposes. Because of the vastness of the oceans as sources of fish, the catching of salt-water fish has been a traditionally free activity and remains so today, although even the sea has its limits, encountered recently in the denudation of stocks by over-fishing, which have led to 'cod wars' and the restriction of fishing freedoms in offshore waters.

Earth and fire − i.e. land for agriculture, residence and recreation; minerals; energy resources − are much less freely available. Apart from sunlight these are, in various degrees, scarce. The days of the frontiersmen and of the caravan trains, finding virgin lands flowing with milk and honey, are now past. The earth is a finite globe. We already know its best places and people are living in all of them.

This brings us to the general question of the allocation of scarce natural resources, which is where economics joins the resource and environmental sciences. In fact, economics can be defined as 'the science which studies human behaviour as a relationship between ends and scarce means which have alternative uses' (L. Robbins, *The Nature and Significance of Economic Science*, 1932). A resource is scarce when it has *utility* (i.e. it can satisfy a need) and at the same time is not available, without effort, to meet this need.

A scarce resource has *value*, which means that people are willing to give up other utilities in order to have some of it. The two primary methods of

1

bringing this about are *bartering,* in which different goods find their relative levels of value through the keenness or reluctance of individual bargainers to exchange one good for another; and *employment,* in which one person gives utility by his own work and, in exchange for these services, receives some other utility.

Money

The invention of money, particularly in the form of standard coins of valuable and stable metals, greatly improved the method of making these exchanges of utility: for example, by enabling the *giving* and *taking* stages of barter to be done separately and independently, through the insertion between them of the two new stages of *selling* and *buying*, in which goods are bartered for *cash*, which is a generalized or *liquid* form of economic value. A *price* is thus simply a value, expressed in money terms.

Originally the value of a coin was literally the value, as an exchangeable resource, of the metal in it. But this had its problems. The discovery of the New World led to a great flow into Europe, in the 16th century, of Spanish–American silver. In most countries at that time silver was the standard coinage metal and, as it became much less scarce as a resource, so its value dropped in relation to goods generally. This is believed to be the main reason for the great *price inflation* of those times, which trebled the prices of goods in much of Europe during the 16th century. There was also the problem of the *debasement* of coinage, which led to *Gresham's law* ('bad money drives out good'). The basis of this was that the payment of cash by *counting* coins, instead of weighing their metal content, tempted people to offer lighter coins, of lower metal content, and hence also tempted others to withdraw the heavier ones from circulation and melt them down.

In the 18th and 19th centuries, growing confidence in the banking system led to the widespread use of paper money and bank notes, on the understanding of their *promissory* nature, i.e. that the person or bank – particularly the state bank – who issued the note would, if called upon to do so, actually pay the promised amount in gold or silver. In the late 19th and early 20th centuries, gold became the generally preferred currency metal and it was a point of economic pride for a country to be *on the gold standard,* i.e. its bank notes could be exchanged for their face value in gold coins. But, already before this, countries had begun inflating their currencies by issuing more paper money than could be backed with metal. The maintenance of public confidence in the value of paper money has in recent times become increasingly a matter of psychology and volatility, which can sometimes lead to wild runaway price inflations. Britain, in severe economic and social difficulty in the early 1930s, came off the gold standard; the effect of subsequent inflations is that a gold sovereign costs about 24 times its face value today.

The Law of Supply and Demand

Adam Smith in the late 18th century and David Ricardo in the early 19th thought that the price of a commodity was governed by the cost (mainly labour cost) of producing it. Thus, if an apple costs as much to grow as a pear, any attempt to hold the market price of apples at twice that of pears would fail, in a *free market economy,* because the much higher gains that could then be made would tempt many pear-growers to produce apples instead, until the market became so glutted that no-one would want apples unless their prices were reduced (see Fig. 1.1). But, if these prices then dropped too far, the growers would give up producing apples until, in the ensuing shortage, customers became willing to bid up the price again through trying to satisfy their need for them. In this way, it was argued, *market forces* in a free economy would always lead prices to match the costs of production.

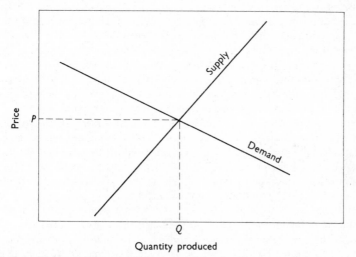

Fig. 1.1 Illustrating the relationship of price to supply and demand. High prices encourage supply and discourage demand; low prices act conversely. Supply and demand come into equilibrium at a certain quantity Q of production and at the corresponding equilibrium price P.

This of course is why it is so hard for a government to intervene successfully in a market economy. The common agricultural policy of the EEC, for example, leads to butter mountains and other gluts or shortages according as the intervention prices are pitched too high or too low. State purchases of products at guaranteed prices, unless accompanied by rigid governmental constraints on the activities of the producers (thus destroying their productive freedom), must lead to great fluctuations in the amounts supplied. If the price is set higher than the production costs, output expands; if set lower, output shrinks; and day-to-day 'fine-tuning' of intervention prices, to find the 'right' level, is useless when, as in farming and most other industries, the decisions and *capital investments* to create new production have to be made months or years before their products can appear on the markets. Technology is not yet able, overnight at a stroke, to turn apples into pears, a fact which some politicians and policy-makers find hard to grasp.

Since Ricardo, the cost theory of prices has split into two very different theories. Marx developed one of them, from the hypothesis that the value of any product is simply the value of the human labour put into producing it, no more and no less. According to this theory the natural environment and its resources have no value of their own, which can hardly appeal to conservationists and primary-producer countries. Very recently, in the aftermath of the 1973 oil crisis, a quite different type of this same *production theory of value* has appeared, which argues that the value of goods should be related to the amount of *energy* consumed in their production. We shall consider these versions of the production theory below.

The other successor to the cost theory veered more radically away from Ricardo, towards a *consumer theory of value.* In the words of the 19th century economist Whately, 'it is not that pearls fetch a high price *because* men have dived for them; but on the contrary, men dive for them because they fetch a high price'. A desperate king, fleeing for his life, once even offered his kingdom for a horse. People who want something badly enough will pay almost any price for it. Today the OPEC group of oil-producing countries, fully alive to the world's present need for their limited product, 'mark up' a selling price 10 to 100 times what it costs to produce this oil and pipe it to the shipping terminals. The value of a scarce natural resource is thus whatever the customer is prepared to pay for it.

But, why is the price of a pearl so much greater than that of a loaf of bread which is vital to life itself? Alfred Marshall's answer, at the end of the 19th century, was that it is *marginal utility,* not *total utility,* that is the demand factor upon which the price depends. Bread has a very high total utility, since it is produced and consumed by mankind in enormous amounts, but the utility of a unit amount of it — of one loaf of bread — which is its *marginal utility,* may nevertheless be small (see Fig. 1.2). The more of a given commodity that a consumer possesses, the less is the extra utility that he gets from buying another unit of it. Ideally, he will stop buying this commodity at the point where the next 'marginal' unit of it would bring him less benefit than spending that same money on something else. Hence it is what he is prepared to pay for a unit at this critical point, i.e. *at the margin*, that determines the unit price of a commodity. The reality of this is shown in the volatility of commodity prices. The production of primary resources such as minerals is rather *inelastic,* i.e. does not in the

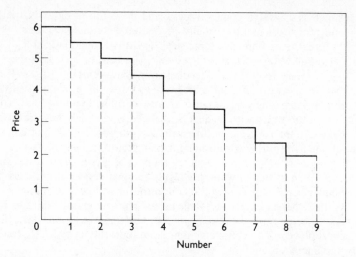

Fig. 1.2 Illustrating marginal utility. A hungry family, with no food, might be willing to pay 6 money units to buy its first loaf of bread. The marginal utility of a loaf is then 6. But if the family already has 8 loaves it may be willing to pay only 2 units for one more. The marginal utility is then 2.

short term change much in response to sudden changes in demand; for example, it takes a long time to open up a new mine. But the demand for such commodities fluctuates suddenly and wildly, with the changing economic fortunes of the consumers, and unwanted stockpiles of a commodity may temporarily build up, on which occasions its marginal utility plummets towards zero.

The Ultimate Resources

Of the various resource factors we have considered, two are outstandingly important: *human effort* and *energy*. The importance of the first is self-evident but that of energy needs some explanation. Energy is the ultimate natural resource in the sense that, if enough of it is available, it can be used to enable all other material goods to be produced. Matter (apart from nuclear transformation) is conserved, so that everything that we do with materials on earth — mining, concentrating and shipping them, purifying them, combining them into new chemical substances, shaping them into usable goods, patching them up, scrapping them when worn out or obsolete — is no more than *cycling* since all these actions are merely a shuffling of the same old bunches of atoms from one place and arrangement to another. Given enough energy and consumer demand, it would in principle be possible to extract all the raw materials needed, if necessary from low-grade sources such as sea water, common rocks, and the debris of old industrial cities; and convert them into virtually any required commodity, which might be an artificial fibre, a chrome steel, a synthetic diamond, a man-made plastic, desalted water, an oasis in the desert, clean air, or even a protein food (e.g. from micro-organisms, feeding on hydrocarbons).

In fact, we have already gone a long way towards this. Modern intensive agriculture is increasingly becoming a means of turning fuel into food. To supply the entire world with fertilizers, at the level at which they are now used in modern intensive agriculture, would require an energy input equal to about one-fifth of the world's present energy output. In a chicken battery, about six times as much energy is put in as is contained in the eggs produced. The desalting of water is a highly energy-intensive process, as also is modern open-cast mining and concentration of low-grade mineral ores. As the richer and more accessible grades get worked out, additional effort has to be put into the mining process. For example, in the USA, the mechanical power used in all metal mines rose fourfold in the 1950s, for the same mineral production.

If energy were as abundant and available as water in a rain-soaked country, the production theory of value would narrow down to a pure labour theory of value, as assumed by Marx, since this energy could then be used unstintingly to extract all useful materials from vast low-grade sources such as sea water. Even the equipment used in producing this energy could itself be all constructed from such extracted materials, so that everything of substance would thus have come from abundant resources of no scarcity value.

There is a slim chance that mankind might eventually get to this point since the earth's energy — for example, from sunlight, hot subterranean rocks, and deuterium in sea water — is enormous compared with all foreseeable needs. But we are several technologies and many years away from this blessed state, as well as being far from solving the problem of how to get rid of all the waste heat without destroying the climate and melting the ice caps.

It is thus important to distinguish between natural *resources* of energy (and other commodities) and *reserves* which are those resources that are economically workable by present technology. The proven reserves of energy are limited and will become still scarcer by the end of the century, as is reflected in the greatly risen prices of oil on world markets. This in turn means that many mineral resources can be extracted economically only from fairly rich and rare deposits, so that these resources also acquire a scarcity value when energy is limited.

For these reasons the consumer theory of value, in which is implied an intrinsic value of scarce resources, is nearer to reality than the production theory under the world conditions of today. Nevertheless, the concept of *added value* (or *net output*) is of great importance for gauging the productive activity of an industry or country. It is equal to the total *revenue* received by the enterprise in return for the sale of its goods and services, minus the cost of the materials, components, energy, etc. that it had to buy as the working substances which it turned into those goods and services. It is thus simply the value which has been added to the throughputs by the processes of production. The total added value for all of a country's activities is the *gross domestic product* (GDP) or *national income* (and, when net income from abroad is included, it is the *gross national product, i.e. GNP*). The word 'gross' here refers to the fact that in the GNP – as distinct from the *net national income* – nothing is subtracted for *depreciation*. All replacement of the stock of *capital equipment,* which has become worn out or obsolete, has to come from the GNP. If all of the GNP is consumed, the country's stock of productive capital equipment is gradually run down. If part of the GNP is invested, this stock may be preserved or even increased.

Cowboys and Spaceships

Traditional economics treats the natural world and its resources with scant respect. Man, his struggles in the market place and factory, occupies the centre of the stage in both free enterprise and Marxist economics. The natural environment has been largely ignored in conventional accounts of the economic process and the earth has been commonly regarded as a free reservoir and bottomless rubbish dump. In the words of K. E. Boulding (*Economics as a Science,* McGraw-Hill, 1970) mankind has operated a 'cowboy' economy – like a reckless exploitation of limitless, empty plains – rather than the 'spaceship' economy that is becoming increasingly necessary on a finite, small and crowded planet. In a cowboy economy, success is measured in terms of the amount of material turned over by its factors of production, whereas in a spaceship economy the criterion for success is not this *turnover* but the maintenance in good order of the existing *capital stocks,* which both in a spaceship and on earth are the inhabitants and their life-support systems. Whereas free enterprise and Marxist economics both lead to the squandering of natural resources, the aim in the *ecological economics* of a spaceship is to conserve, maintain, use and use again. This kind of economics has hardly begun to appear in the textbooks, yet. When it does, its effects on the course of economic thinking will be profound, for the focus then will be on the easing of the demand on natural resources by maintaining the quality of life in a less wasteful way.

Ever since Adam Smith, it has been a leading idea of economics that the individual, in acting for his own gain, is led by an 'invisible hand' to promote the general interest. The first convincing demonstration that the economics of the 'general interest' is quite fundamentally different from the micro-economics of the individual came with Keynes's 'General Theory' which showed that, whereas an individual Micawber might cure his economic depression by spending less, for a whole nation the right answer could sometimes be to spend *more*. But Keynes's theory was directed towards unemployment, not to the environment and natural resources. There are, nevertheless, similarly contrary features in ecological economics; they go by the name of *external diseconomies*.

Consider, for example, the problem of the common pasture land declared free for general public use in mediaeval England (see G. Hardin, 'The Tragedy of the Commons', *Science,* volume 162, page 1243, 1968). If a herdsman increases his stock by one animal, grazing on that common land, he then gets its full direct benefit minus the effect of the loss of overall grazing quality due to the burden of this extra mouth which the commons has to feed. But this particular loss is hardly felt by the herdsman in question since its burden is shared amongst everyone using the commons. Hence he has an overwhelming incentive to increase his stock; and again and again. And so has *every other* herdsman on the commons. The commons may thus be destroyed by overgrazing, lack of care, and erosion, in which event all the herdsmen are ruined by the totality of their actions which, individually for each one of them considered alone, is undoubtedly in his own best interest. The external diseconomy, i.e. the penalty to others of an individual act, may be small but when everyone is induced to act similarly, the totality of these diseconomies may lead to ruin.

There are many modern examples of this, mostly to do with the finiteness of the natural environment. The discharge of polluting wastes into a neighbour's living space, the depopulation of the seas by over-fishing, the blighting of national parks by over-use, the aggravation of commodity shortages due to panic buying and hoarding of all remaining stocks, are typical. They set Society some extremely difficult problems of regulation: whether the rationing should be done by dividing the finite resources up in the form of private property, as in the enclosures of the land in 19th century England; or by the imposition of a tax on their use; or by central government control which restricts individual freedom; in every case this remains a difficult problem which, if improperly solved, can lead to the destruction of a source of benefit through its very scarcity. Whatever the form of the social solution, it has to be one that recognizes that the resource, being finite and exhaustible in extent, thereby has *value* and because of this must be *priced,* in some form or other, so as to restrict its consumption and to pay for its care and maintenance.

There is also a physical reason why natural resources have an intrinsic value. Matter is conserved; all the atoms that enter an economic system as raw materials eventually leave it as waste. Energy also is conserved (apart from nuclear transformations); the amount that enters an economic system, in the long run, equals the amount that leaves it. This is true of the entire earth, which keeps its temperature constant by radiating out into space almost exactly as much energy as it receives from the sun. The question then is: how is it possible for Man to produce something *material,* given the fact that he cannot produce either matter or energy? (N. Georgescu-Roegen,

'Economics and Entropy', *The Ecologist,* Volume 2, page 13, 1972). The answer lies in the *quality* of energy. The highest quality is that energy we call *work;* the lowest is lukewarm *heat.* Work is energy that produces mechanical change. Work can be all turned into heat — for example by friction — but only a fraction of heat can be turned into work (in a heat engine), so that all processes have an *irreversible* character in that the overall changes in quality of energy they may produce are *always* downwards. The second law of thermodynamics expresses just this fact, although in the language of *entropy* (which is the negative of quality).

The high-temperature energy received from the sun is of higher quality than the low-temperature energy the earth radiates back into space. Most of the quality of this sunlight is wasted by the earth's natural processes, becoming low-temperature heat, but some is preserved, particularly in plants, animals, and fossil fuels. All living processes, all economic activities, are examples of thermodynamic *engines* which consume high-quality energy, convert some of it to high-grade products such as biological cells and motor cars, and throw away the rest as low-grade heat. This ultimate resource of high-quality energy is supplied by the sun in amounts far beyond Man's present needs, but little of it is accessible in concentrated form and so it is a scarce resource, for active mammals, whether embodied in fuel, food, or material goods. In this situation, the degradation of energy from high quality to low, in its passage through an economic system, represents a real and permanent loss of value. The aim of a spaceship economy is to maintain the fabric and inhabitants of the ship in good order, while mini-mizing this loss of intrinsic value. In principle, new technology could, by continually increasing the availability to Man of the earth's high-quality energy, make it unnecessary to adopt a spaceship economy for the fore-seeable future. Indeed, much present-day energy research is aimed at achieving just this, but many of the problems are so severe that it would be unwise to pin the entire future on the possibility of technological success.

2 Energy

The Shadow of Malthus

Nature is bountiful. The fact that a country's consumption of such a basic resource as energy has not in the past usually exceeded about 2% of its GNP simply reflects that energy has been an abundant and hence cheap resource. Even though mankind has so far learned to tap only a minute amount of the high-quality energy with which the earth is provided, this has been sufficiently large relative to the need as to make fuel almost as available as air and water.

The industrialized and prosperous societies in the western world were built up on the basis of cheap coal, the sheer abundance of which implanted in them a long-lasting and still continuing wasteful attitude towards the use of energy, as is shown by the neglect of thermal insulation in many houses and buildings, and in the growing popularity of electricity as a convenient form of energy for space heating, even though two-thirds of the energy of the primary fuel is lost in its generation and distribution.

After the second World War, at a time when people were beginning to feel anxious about future coal supplies, because of the growing and understandable dislike of coal mining as a human occupation, nature proved even more bountiful. The truly enormous extent of certain oil fields, mainly in the Middle East, became apparent. The cost of tapping, shipping and using this oil was irresistibly low. Cheap coal gave way to still cheaper oil. User upon user, industry upon industry, country upon country, became more and more dependent on oil, so that today this provides almost half of the world's energy consumption, as shown in Table 2.1.

Table 2.1 World Energy Production (mtce*)

(Source: *UN Statistics on World Energy Supplies*)

Year	Coal	Oil	Natural gas	Nuclear, hydro and geothermal electricity	Total
1950	1605	700	261	41	2607
1960	2191	1396	622	86	4295
1970	2398	3004	1432	157	6990
1972	2430	3350	1630	175	7585

* Mtce = millions of tons of coal-equivalent. One ton of oil is typical equivalent to about 1.7 tons of coal.

As countries' GNPs have risen, so also has their energy consumption (see Fig. 2.1), which has been used in increasingly profligate ways, for example in unlimited private motoring, higher central heating temperatures, and all-electric houses. Since 1950 world energy consumption has grown *exponentially*, i.e. according to the law of compound interest (see Appendix 1 to Chapter 2), at about 5% a year. On the basis of the (slightly approximate) *doubling time* formula, $70/g$, where g is the annual percentage growth, the amount consumed in a year has thus been *doubling* every 14 years. World consumption of oil and natural gas has grown even faster, at about 7.8% a year, i.e. doubling every 9 years.

And so the awful warning of Malthus, reaching out across the years from 1798, about the dangers of growing exponentially on a limited resource base, went unheeded until the great oil crisis of 1973, which produced a quadrupling of crude oil prices within a few months. Admittedly, the

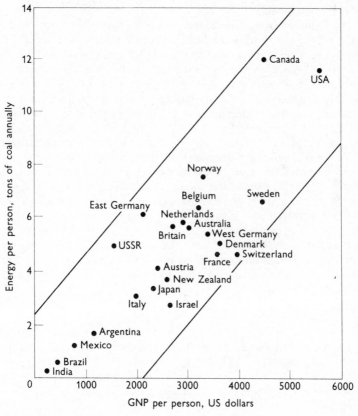

Fig. 2.1 The relation between use of energy and Gross National Product, per person, in various countries.

immediate cause of this was political, but nevertheless it could never have happened, at least in that severe way, if oil resources around the world were as truly abundant, widely distributed and immediately accessible, as the world's galloping oil consumption required.

The year 1973 is thus a landmark in the world's economic history, the year of the sharp transition from cheap energy to the pricing up of energy as a scarce resource. And where oil led the way other resources followed, either because their producers saw similar opportunities, through scarcity, or because the energy cost in producing them had multiplied devastatingly. Thus, whereas in 1972 the world's total deliveries of fuel, raw materials and food, stood at about $150 billion*, compared with trade in all goods of some $400 billion, by 1974 the same amount of fuel, materials and food was costing $320 billion, a truly massive increase, the effect of which has been felt throughout the economies of the consumer countries in the form of inflation, balance of payments deficits, recession, unemployment, and fall in living standards.

The transition from cheap energy, and other natural resources, to price levels that reflect a full awareness of their scarcity value, is setting the consumer countries economical and social problems of immense severity and it is still hard even now to see the ultimate political repercussions of the transition. We must leave this wider question, however, to consider the more specific problem of the future supply of and demand for energy. Economists tend to underrate the technical difficulties of squaring demand and supply, by dismissing the problem with an airy remark 'the market forces will look after all that', implying that there are *price elasticities* in the amounts supplied and demanded; in other words, if the demand is at first greater than the supply, the advantage of bargaining will lie with the suppliers, who will then be able to raise prices, which will in turn stimulate greater supplies and reduced consumption, by various measures, until a balance is struck between supply and demand at a new *equilibrium* price level. There is of course much to be said for this argument, but it has the great weakness of overlooking the technical difficulties and time required in making such re-adjustments. Rome was not built in a day; and in the energy field it can take 20 to 50 years to bring about a major innovation in the supply industry.

Fuel Supplies

In the days when *oil* could be bought for less than $3 a barrel† from the low-cost oilfields, its price undercut almost all other major fuels (except of course locally gathered firewood and peat). But the fourfold price rise in 1973—4 and further rises since then have made it possible for many

---

* One billion = 1 000 000 000.
† 10 barrels are approximately $1\frac{1}{3}$ metric tons

other sources of oil, previously ruled out because of higher production costs — for example, more complete extraction from existing fields; opening up of small, or offshore, or remote, oil fields; production of oil from tar sands, shales, coal and wood — to enter the market competitively. Already by 1973 it had been estimated that oil could be produced from offshore fields, tar sands or coal at not more than $7 per barrel (although of course, with general inflation, all prices have risen since then). But a new market opportunity is not instantly realizable. Several years of preliminary work are necessary to bring a new source into production. Offshore oil requires vast marine engineering structures, which cost much time and money to install. The capital investment needed for producing North Sea oil, for example, is about $5000 per daily barrel of oil produced. The present requirement in Britain is about 2 million barrels daily, thus calling for an investment of about $10 billion. The raising and spending of this amount of money, in the North Sea, is a 5 to 10 year task. Some of the other new sources, such as oil produced from other substances, will take still longer to bring into being because they also require new technology, thus involving scientific research and technical development, as well as capital investment and engineering construction. Major new oil sources could thus not come fully into service before the 1980s, even though the price level has left the way wide open for them ever since 1974.

The world's *proven reserves* (i.e. fully established by drilling to be economically recoverable with present technology and prices) in oil fields in 1974 amounted to about 750 billion barrels, whereas its *ultimate resources* (i.e. which might be recoverable with future technology and prices) from oil fields were estimated at about 2000 billion barrels. Present world oil consumption is about 20 billion barrels per year, so that at this rate the proven oilfield reserves will last nearly 40 years and the ultimate resources (if they exist!) about 100 years. But of course these periods will be seriously curtailed if the world's oil consumption grows in future at anything like the rate of the 1960s. For example, at 4% annual growth of consumption, starting at the present rate, even the ultimate resources would be consumed within 40 years.

In addition to these oil field resources, various *tar sands* and *shales* could provide perhaps even as much as 5000 billion barrels, after some considerable technological and engineering development. Moreover, if it becomes possible to convert *coal* to oil economically then the amount producible, e.g. at 3 barrels per ton of coal, could expand to the scale of the world's coalfield deposits which, as we shall see below, are very large. It seems then that at prices ranging from $10 to $20 a barrel (at 1976 costs) and with the necessary technological, financial and engineering development, the world's foreseeable oil needs could be met, reasonably adequately, for the next 50 years; but such developments will need to take over from the present-day major oil sources at about the end of this century if the impending world oil shortage due to the coming exhaustion of the latter is to be avoided, and as soon as possible if problems due to the geographically uneven distribution of the oilfield resources are to be avoided.

Estimated world amounts of *natural gas,* whether as proven reserves or ultimate resources, usually lie within half or two-thirds of those of oilfield oil. Technically, it may be rather easier to turn coal into *synthetic natural gas* (or, equivalently, to methanol or hydrogen) than into oil. If so then, since natural gas is as good a fuel as oil, were oil from coal to become economically attractive, so would gas from coal. In that case, synthetic natural gas could, if required, be produced on a scale limited only by the availability of coal.

In highly developed countries *coal* has become less popular as a fuel, partly because oil has been so cheap and partly for social reasons. But the world's proven reserves and ultimate resources of coal are 5 to 10 times larger than those of oil and natural gas. On any reasonable projection of future world trends, these coal resources are sufficient to last throughout the 21st century. Indeed, now that oil prices have greatly risen, interest in coal has revived and it seems possible that coal may become the main source of the world's energy in the early years of the 21st century. But there are difficulties. Coal, while more widely distributed than oil, is nevertheless far from uniformly spread. Even Western Europe, which used traditionally to run itself entirely on its own coal, could hardly hope now to provide more than about one-quarter of its future energy needs from its own coal resources. Furthermore, in 30 years' time men can hardly be expected, in a world of automation, to accept work underground at a coal face. New technology for remote coal mining will thus be needed, as well as means for treating the coal afterwards to remove its sulphur and to turn it into more generally usable forms of fuel.

The other significant fuel today is *uranium,* for nuclear power stations. The economics of nuclear power are dominated by the *capital cost* of the reactor station (see below), but fuel cost does play a major part in relation to the abundance of nuclear fuel. In natural uranium only one atom in 140 is capable of undergoing nuclear fission in a *non-breeder* type of reactor (such as the commercial ones in use or under construction in 1976), so that the amounts of uranium ore required are much larger than would appear simply from the energy of atomic fission.

The nuclear reactors already operating or soon to be in service world wide will need over 1.2 million tons of uranium by the end of this century, which is more than the 1.0 million tons which have been estimated could be mined at a cost of up to $15/lb of uranium oxide. However, a doubling of reactor fuel costs, which would still be only a small part of total reactor costs, would enable mining costs to be raised fourfold and this would enable many more deposits to be worked economically. For example, it has been estimated that, at $50/lb, nearly 7 million tons of uranium could be extracted (USAEC, *Nuclear Fuel Supply,* WASH–1242, 1973).

The other main type of fission reactor, the *breeder*, can in principle use up to 60 times as many of the natural uranium atoms (after conversion to plutonium) as the non-breeder reactor. For such a reactor even a natural uranium cost of, say, $200/lb would be tolerable, which is high enough to allow uranium to be extracted economically even from sea water, if necessary, thus opening the way to virtually unlimited fuel supplies.

Cutting the Fuel Bill

In thirsting for energy, Man suffers the torment of Tantalus. There is far more than we need, beyond our reach. As we have seen, one answer is to let fuel prices rise to the level at which it pays to produce fuel from some of the larger costlier sources. But there is another, quite opposite, answer. It is to invest in *capital equipment* which can deal with a lot of the energy need at a small or even zero fuel cost. The breeder reactor provides a modern example, but the traditional ones go back to windmills, water wheels, and woollens.

Such schemes fall into two groups. In the first are those for tapping the earth's really vast energy sources and permanent energy flows; for example, solar energy, neutron breeder and fusion nuclear power, water power including waves and tides, winds and geothermal energy. In the second group are the schemes for *conservation*, in which the aim is not to deny energy needs but to satisfy them with less consumption of energy. Examples are district heating with waste heat, improved thermal efficiency of industrial processes, insulation of houses, heat pumps, warm clothing, bicycles and public transport.

The various merits of these, some of which are hardly developed as yet, are being fiercely debated at the present time. From the purely economic standpoint, however, they can be judged simply as various options for *capital investment* in terms of the amount of *return on capital* each can earn, i.e. in this case the energy bills saved. The energy saved per unit investment is of course only one of the factors which enter into the *cost-benefit* analysis by which particular options are selected. There are many others, such as safety, reliability, convenience, cleanliness, adaptability, and independence, also to be considered; and some of the more expensive options may offer these in greater measure. Their additional benefits have to be set against the additional capital outlays necessary to acquire them and then judged in the light of their *opportunity costs,* i.e. the value of other utilities which have to be foregone to pay for the chosen option.

Even for the well-established energy systems, the calculation of the return on investment is a complex procedure, which requires good judgement when making assumptions about the many uncertainties involved, particularly those to do with future changes in demand, costs, prices, interest rates, and public acceptability. High interest rates particularly discourage those capital investments whose benefits accrue only over a long period of time (see Appendix 2 to Chapter 2) and so they are unfavourable to long-term conservation schemes and to spaceship economics generally. For schemes still at the experimental stage there are the still greater uncertainties of whether and when they will become technically successful at commercial prices.

The expected return on capital varies enormously between systems. At one extreme there is the simple lining of the roof-space of a house with glass wool to keep the heat in, at a ratio of capital cost to energy saved of about $150/kilowatt (thermal)*, giving an annual return on capital of over 50% in terms of saving on heating bills. At the other extreme is solar electricity generated from photovoltaic cells, as in spacecraft, at about $20 000/kW (electrical), although strenuous efforts are now being made to develop solar–electric cells at much lower costs. Between these extremes, several of the other systems such as nuclear power, wave, wind and tidal power, have cost–energy ratios of the general order of $1000/kW (electrical).

Energy Accounting

A pure energy–cost theory of value cannot be generally valid since the energy used in producing manufactured goods generally accounts for less than 5% of their total production cost (although it is much higher for primary materials such as steel and aluminium). But energy accounting, i.e. analysing the energy flows in the production of goods, is nevertheless important, particularly as a starting point for planning conservation pro- grammes. At the national level the percentages of primary fuel input which flow into the various sectors of the economy are typically about as follows:

Sector	Per cent
Domestic	30
Materials production	30
Other industries	15
Transport	15
Services	6
Agriculture	4

The scope for energy conservation is clearly greatest in the domestic sector. The consumption here is very large and the greater part of it is used in providing low-quality heat for space heating. A domestic *heat pump*, for example, ought to be able to provide three times as much energy, as low- quality heat, than it consumes in the high-quality form as electricity.

---

* The energy content in 1 ton of domestic coal is about 8000 kilowatt hours (thermal). This is not the same as electrical energy, however, because electrical is of higher quality than thermal. A modern coal-fired power station generates about 2500 kilowatt hours (electrical) per ton of coal burnt.

The materials sector is of course a big consumer because it produces primary materials in great bulk, in many cases by energy-intensive processes. Simply because energy thereby is a big factor in the production cost of many such materials (e.g. 20% of the total cost of steel) energy conservation has already been long practised in these industries. The overall energy consumption in going from iron ore to finished steel is about ten times the room-temperature oxidation energy of iron, which implies an overall thermodynamic efficiency of order 10%, a rather good figure for such a complex sequence of high-temperature operations.

For engineering equipment generally, and similar products such as motor vehicles, the energy consumed in the materials and processes of construction typically amounts to about 20 000 kilowatt hours per ton of equipment. This raises an interesting question about the economics of energy production and supply. The high capital cost of many energy systems is due to the large and complex engineering equipment that they require. Since energy is consumed in the production of this equipment, is there a possibility that the energy input may *exceed* the energy output? A typical calculation of this kind has been made for a non-breeder nuclear power station of 1000 megawatts capacity (P. Chapman, *Fuel's Paradise,* Penguin Special, 1975). In this case, assuming 25 years of operation on uranium mined from 0.3% ores, a total energy equivalent to about 10 000 million kilowatt hours (thermal) is consumed in producing about 110 000 million kilowatt hours of electricity. This is a very large return, 10 to 1, on the energy investment. However, if the station had to run on uranium produced from much lower grade ores (e.g. below 0.002%), the energy consumed in mining could exceed that produced by the system. This sets a limit to the grades of ore usable by such reactors, and it rules out the truly vast uranium sources such as granite and sea water. This limit does not apply of course to the breeder type of reactor.

Considering the 10 to 1 case further, because five or more years are usually required to construct and commission a large power station, the energy flow is *negative* initially; a positive return is not gained until well after the investment is begun. The *present value* of the energy return which will eventually be gained has thus to be partially *discounted* to allow for the fact that its benefits are deferred. Although expressed in terms of energy flows, this is of course no more than the familiar principle of *cash flow* in a financial investment, in which the present value of a cash return has to be discounted, at a rate set by the current level of interest rates, by a factor that grows like compound interest according as the date of the return lies farther off in the future (see Appendix 2 to Chapter 2). But it sets an upper limit to the rate of constructing stations if this construction is required not to take all the energy coming from the already existing stations.

It is interesting to consider such a reactor, not in its nuclear role, but as a somewhat unusual method of using *fossil* fuel for the generation of electricity. As regards this fossil fuel, e.g. coal or oil, there is then a choice of how it might be so used. In a conventional way, we might put the above 10 000 million kW h (thermal) of input energy into the construction and fuelling of a fossil fuel power station. From past experience we could obtain about 2500 million kW h (electrical). In the unusual way, we could use some of it to build a nuclear station and the rest of it to mine and prepare its uranium fuel. On the 10 to 1 basis outlined above, we could then obtain 110 000 million kW h (electrical). Thus fossil fuel, if applied to a nuclear system on this basis, can enable 40 times more electricity to be generated!

Conclusion

For most of the world the days of cheap, abundant, energy have now gone and, on foreseeable technology, will not return. Nevertheless the world can have all the energy it wants, by paying higher prices and by getting the necessary new technologies and industries ready in good time. In broad terms it can pay either higher fuel costs or higher capital investment, but in both cases the cash flows will have to be very large and the consequential shift of major financial resources into energy will leave appreciably less for other purposes, so that the general rate of world economic growth will be limited appreciably by the rise in price of energy.

These effects will not be spread evenly across the world. Some countries have both wealth and abundant indigenous energy; some have one only of these; some have neither. The international cash flows across the world's energy markets are already very large and have a considerable impact on world trade.

It is important here to make a distinction between *low-cost* energy, at a price which has been artificially pushed high and the purchase of which merely shifts wealth from buyers to sellers; and, on the other hand, intrinsically *high-cost* energy the financing of which necessarily leads to general loss of opportunities for other things. The world has recently moved from *low-price, low-cost,* energy to *high-price, low-cost,* energy and all the signs are that it will soon have to get used to *high-price, high-cost* energy.

Appendix 1   Exponential Growth

If a unit of money is banked at an interest rate of $100r\%$ a year, which is compounded annually, its value grows to $N_1 = (1 + r)$ units after the first year, to $N_2 = N_1(1 + r) = (1 + r)^2$ after the second, and to $N_n = (1 + r)^n$ after the nth year. This is the *law of compound interest*. If this same annual interest is compounded s times a year, the expression becomes

$$N_n = \left(1 + \frac{r}{s}\right)^{sn}$$

If it is compounded *continuously*, i.e. if $s \rightarrow \infty$, the sum N_t after a time t (years) is then

$$N_t = \left(1 + \frac{r}{s}\right)^{st} = \left[\left(1 + \frac{r}{s}\right)^{\frac{s}{r}}\right]^{rt} = e^{rt},$$

where $e = \lim_{x \rightarrow 0}(1 + x)^{1/x}$ is the *exponential* symbol, or base of natural logarithms, approximately equal to 2.718. The *law of exponential growth*, e^{rt}, applies to any quantity (e.g. the number of individuals in a growing population) which increases by a constant percentage of the total in a constant period of time.

The simplest way to appreciate exponential growth is through the concept of the *doubling* time. We can rewrite $N_t = e^{rt}$ in (natural) logarithmic form as $rt = \ln N_t$. The time for the quantity to double (i.e. $N_t = 2$) is thus

$$t = \frac{\ln 2}{r} = \frac{0.6931}{r}.$$

Hence if $g\ (= 100r)$ is the annual $\%$ growth or $\%$ interest, the doubling time is approximately $70/g$ years.

Appendix 2 Discounted Present Value

If a fixed sum of money is to be given at a certain date in the future, then its *present value* to the recipient is smaller than if it were given to him immediately since he is denied the benefit of its earning interest in the meantime. Thus the present value of 1000 units to be received in n years time is $1000/(1 + r)^n$, when the interest rate is $100r\%$ a year. Some examples of present values are as follows:

Years before receipt:	0	1	5	10	20	50
Interest rate 5%:	1000	952	784	614	377	87
10%:	1000	909	621	386	149	9
15%:	1000	870	497	247	61	1

For example if the interest (or discount) rate is 10%, then 1000 units to be received in 5 years time have a present value of 621, because 621 units invested today at this rate of compound interest could grow to 1000 units in 5 years.

3 Minerals

Galloping Consumption

Six minerals – oil, gas, coal, iron (steel), aluminium and copper – account for two-thirds of the world's consumption of mineral resources. Of the remaining one-third, almost half is accounted for by sand, gravel and stone, which are abundant, have no scarcity value, only a production and delivery cost, and are not much traded internationally. No other mineral accounts individually for more than about 1% of world mineral consumption. The consumption of all mineral resources amounted in the 1960s to only about 4.5% of the total value of the world's economic output and about one-half of this was taken up with energy resources. The importance of mineral resources is much greater than these small figures represent, for they provide the raw materials whose properties – strength, energy content, electrical conductivity, lightness, corrosion resistance, etc. – keep the wheels of modern society turning. To the user, a material is merely a substance which fills a given space with certain required properties, at a price – for example, a coping stone, cylinder block, window pane, dental filling – and one material can be *substituted* for another provided its properties are satisfactory.

The great modern consumption of materials was started by the Industrial Revolution. From the late 18th century to the end of the 19th the world's consumption of minerals rose ten times (during which period its population doubled). Since then, the pace has increased still more dramatically. In the 70 years up to 1970 the annual consumption grew 12.5 times, in cash terms (adjusted to constant 1972 prices) from $13 billion to $166 billion. For each person in the world today, about 8 tons of earth are taken each year and 3.3 tons of this are used as constructional materials, 2.5 tons are waste, 1.7 tons go into fuels, and the remaining 0.5 tons provide 300 lbs of metals and 340 lbs of non-metals.

The rates of world consumption have been increasing so sharply for so long – e.g. at about 4% a year for metals such as steel, copper and zinc, i.e. doubling in less than 20 years; and even higher for aluminium, cement and phosphate (5 to 10% a year) – that such galloping consumption has roused many fears that the world's supply of minerals may soon be exhausted. One of the most complete expressions of these, in the book *The Limits to Growth* (D. H. Meadows, et al., Potomac Associates Universe Books, New York, 1972), gave the following figures:

21

	Years of availability at present rates of usage	Average growth in usage, % per year	Years of availability with growing usage
Aluminium	100	6.4	31 (55)
Iron	240	1.8	93 (173)
Copper	36	4.6	21 (48)
Nickel	150	3.4	53 (96)
Lead	26	2.0	21 (64)
Zinc	23	2.9	18 (50)
Tin	17	1.1	15 (61)
Tungsten	40	2.5	28 (72)
Mercury	13	2.6	13 (41)

The primary source of these figures was *Mineral Facts and Figures* (US Bureau of Mines, 1970). The figures in the last column were calculated on the assumption of continuing exponential growth at the annual rates given in the middle column; the figures in brackets show the effect of assuming the availability of five times as much reserves as are known at present. We see that the estimated years of availability are disturbingly short, for all except iron.

No Physical Limits

However, the primary statistics upon which these estimates were based refer to *current known reserves of mineral located in deposits economically workable at present prices by present technology*. These qualifications make an enormous difference, as is shown by the fact that, according to previous estimates of the years of availability, most of the above metals would have gone by now. Tin, for example, was given only 10 more years of availability in 1929. Physically, of course, there is no question of exhausting these minerals. Quite apart from the fact that their atoms are physically conserved, so that all we do is to move them from one place to another, the amounts in the mineable layers of the earth and in the oceans are truly stupendous; there is enough in these for example to provide everyone on earth with a personal $2\frac{1}{2}$ ton chariot of pure gold. There is thus no question of any truly physical scarcity of such minerals. Any scarcity in practice is an *economic scarcity*. What matters is the cost of producing the materials in relation to the demand. Moreover, since there is little economic incentive in incurring the costs of explorations to find deposits that will not be needed for 20 or more years ahead, the years of availability of *known* reserves may hover more or less permanently at around this value, quite independently of physical availability or rates of consumption.

If prices rise then marginally poorer deposits, i.e. potential reserves not previously included in the currently known list, become economically workable; and the total of such listed reserves is immediately increased, even if no new deposits are found. Conversely, if prices fall, some marginally economic mines may be forced to stop working; but their removal from the list of current known reserves does not mean that the minerals in them have vanished! It is thus often said about minerals production that 'the problem is always one of economics, not of geology'. For example, if the price of copper were to double, then the output from *existing* mines might be quadrupled, quite apart from further possibilities from new ones.

Such relations between economic output and price are defined by the *elasticity of supply* index. For example, an index of 1 means that a 1% increase in mineral price can bring forth a 1% increase in rate of production; and an index of 2 means that this same price rise can bring forth a 2% increase in production. Uranium has one of the highest values, about 11, indicating that the amount of reserves rises steeply with price. Most of the common non-ferrous metals have values in the range of 1 to 2.

With a sufficient expenditure, particularly of energy (see Fig. 3.1), the amounts of mineral that could be extracted become virtually limitless. It would be possible for example to produce aluminium from clay. The limit

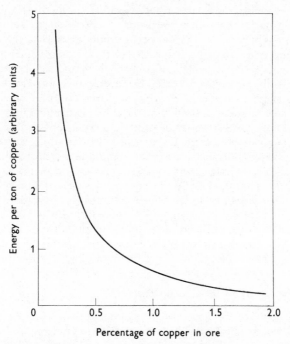

Fig. 3.1 By the expenditure of increasingly large amounts of energy, per ton of copper produced, increasingly low-grade ores may be mined (based on P. Chapman, *Fuel's Paradise,* Penguin, 1975).

in the current known reserves of this geologically abundant metal stems from the fact that the present source of it is the less abundant ore, *bauxite*. But by using even more energy than now, we could extract aluminium from the vast sources of common clay. Similarly for other minerals. Given enough energy, we could extract all we need, if necessary by grinding up ordinary rocks or chemically from sea water.

The lack of cheap abundant energy makes this unrealistic, quite apart from other problems. Only for a few minerals, e.g. metals such as iron, aluminium, and magnesium, are the concentrations in rocks or sea water large enough for extraction from them to be a serious prospect in the present economic and technological state of the world. The average abundance of most other metals, in the earth's crust, is one-thousandth or less of that in the lowest grade current reserves, so that the amounts of energy required and tonnages of rock to be crushed, worked over and then dumped, would be prohibitively vast, on present technology. For the sea also, the extremely low concentrations of most dissolved minerals mean that enormous volumes of water would need to be processed. For example, it has been estimated that, to produce 400 tons of zinc a year — a pretty small output — the extractive plant would have to handle an amount equivalent to the combined flows of the Hudson and Delaware rivers.

Nevertheless, there are some metals such as copper and nickel whose concentrations in general rocks are within striking distance of the present cut-off grades of ore deposits. Some igneous rocks, for example, contain several hundred parts per million of copper, which is about one-tenth of the lowest presently workable ore grades. However, geologists warn that, for many substances, there is a difference in kind between the mineral deposits which are now mined — and which will be exhausted in the foreseeable future — and the much lower-grade widely dispersed deposits that make up much of the potential reserves. Economists tend to overlook the geological facts when they assume that there exists a continuous sequence of deposits, ranging gradually from scarce high-grade to vast low-grade ones. Only for a few types of deposit, such as the porphyry copper ores, is it possible for example to apply the *Lasky Rule* which states that the tonnage of ore increases geometrically as the grade of ore falls arithmetically. In contrast, for many types of deposit there is an abrupt transition from rich ore to barren rock and in such cases 'lowering the grade' often means merely diluting the same limited amount of good ore with more barren rock.

Running Faster to stay in the same Place

Just as the height of the next wave, on a beach, gives no clue as to the height of the next tide, so the daily ups-and-downs of commodity prices provide no basis for predicting the long-term trends. If we smooth out the short-term changes, what then emerges is the apparent absence of any effects of scarcity on price, over many years. For over a century now, in the USA, the prices in real terms of most minerals have slowly declined (at least until recently), even though production has increased many times and most of the richer mines of the 19th century have become worked out. For example, at the turn of the century copper mining was based on deposits that averaged 5% copper, whereas today the figure is down to about 0.6% and still falling; nevertheless the world price of copper fell from about 40 cents a pound in 1900 to 20 cents a pound in 1933 (all measured in 1957 dollars) and has only in the last few years risen sharply upward, to about 60 cents a pound.

The explanation of this long-term insensitivity of mineral prices lies in the qualifying words 'by present technology' in the definition of current known reserves. Technology is changing all the time, making possible today the economic working of deposits unthinkable a few years ago. Technology has been able in general to more than hold its own, so enabling prices to stay steady despite increasing demands and the exhaustion of the richest lodes. There is in fact a delicate running balance between technology and demand. Increasing demand and advancing technology both make the working of lower-grade deposits possible, but they achieve their effect in opposite ways; the first through the possibility of higher prices, the second through the promise of lower costs. The actual trend of long-term market prices then depends on the running balance between them. If the technology runs ahead of the demand and the using up of existing known reserves, then the stock of unused economic reserves increases and the price falls in consequence. And conversely, if the technology lags behind, the prices rise. The long-term price trend shows that, for most of the past century, the technology has been slightly ahead. For most minerals (although not recently for oil) the position seems to be that the technological capabilities and the amounts of potential reserves both act as large buffers on the long-term price levels, helping to stabilize them.

Will this state of affairs continue? It seems likely that technology will be able to hold its own, in the face of gradual changes in demand and qualities of deposit, provided that energy is not a major constraint. On the other hand, environmental problems are likely to be an important limitation, since the newer mining technologies are mainly concerned with the open-cast digging of large low-grade deposits, which means that large areas of land are worked over and mountains of spoil created. One potential technology which would not suffer this disadvantage is the recovery from the deep ocean bed of *manganese nodules,* which exist in large numbers and are rich sources of several non-ferrous metals.

Making the Most of Things

Even if minerals technology and the sizes of incipiently workable deposits prove inadequate in future to enable demand to be met at constant prices, other factors can come into play to dampen long-term price rises, by abating the demand for scarce or expensive materials.

Since it is *properties,* not the material as such, that the end user wants, there is usually an opportunity to *substitute* one material for another, insofar as the technological and economic factors allow this. There is of course already a good deal of substitution. Aluminium has replaced copper for electrical cables. Plastics have taken over from wood and metals in many household goods. We are fortunate in that the main property wanted in those materials that are used in really large amounts, i.e. *mechanical strength,* is available in several of the most common and securely available ones. In fact, steel, cement, and timber, all have similarly high strength/cost ratios and so are fairly substitutable, one for another, in the construction industry.

There are nevertheless some basic technical limits to substitution. Some substances have exceptional properties, which are not easily imitated by others. Tin remains supreme for sliding bearings; chromium for corrosion-resistance; silver for photographic emulsion; tungsten for high-speed cutting tools; platinum metals for catalysts; mercury for amalgams; tetraethyl lead for anti-knock petrol; potash and phosphates for agriculture; and fluorspar for steelmaking. If one of these suddenly became very scarce or expensive, the economists' rule that a substitute would then inevitably appear might fail through Man's technological inabilities. Furthermore, the substitution of one material for another simply increases the demand for the new one, which may also be limited in supply. The substitution of plastics for many other household materials, which is of course a great recent world trend, increases the demand for petrochemicals and these have to be made from the world's diminishing resources of oil and natural gas. Plastics might in future be made from coal, but this is not generally economic on present technology.

A second way of abating the demand on primary resources is by *recycling,* i.e. by retrieving wastes and feeding them back as inputs into the productive system. This is of course no new thing. Many fine buildings have been built from the stones and bricks of their predecessors. The waste from old gravity-separation gold washings has been worked over and over again, first using the mercury amalgam method of extracting gold; then using the cyanide method; and now often again to extract uranium. In Britain the scrap-metal industry became of critical importance in the last war and is now a major industry. About 50% of its steel and 40% of its non-ferrous metals now comes from recycled scrap. More generally, 1 million tons of copper were recycled from scrap during 1970, in North America, Europe and Japan, as well as the 2 million tons that were directly recycled during manufacturing processes.

Recycling is mainly a labour-intensive activity, not requiring much capital or energy. For this reason, the high and growing cost of labour has traditionally limited its scope. If energy and capital become relatively scarcer, in future, then recycling will be economically favoured. Moreover, there will then be an incentive to design future manufactured goods so that they can be taken apart more easily into sorted scrap, after use. Against these trends, however, is the fact that some materials are being used, particularly domestically, in increasingly dispersed forms – for example, fine copper wire or aluminium foil – and the cost of collecting and sorting these is high. Moreover, where there is rapidly increasing consumption, recycling can make only a partial contribution because it necessarily can only work on the remains of the past, more limited, outputs.

Finally, there is the more *economic use* of materials. Again, much of this happens through the normal effect of market forces. Where substitution is possible, rival materials industries will seek to gain competitive advantages against one another by offering their materials, or the properties belonging to them, at lower cost. The great size of modern industrial plants is simply a response to the surface-to-volume scaling laws so as to get more output per ton of process plant. Again, all the recent scientific development of strong materials, which has greatly increased the strength-to-weight ratios of engineering constructions, is a direct contribution to the more economic use of materials, even though the motivation for such developments is usually expressed in terms of better engineering performance.

On the other hand, as consumers in modern society, we generally prefer convenience to economy. Private motoring is preferred to public transport because it takes us door-to-door at our own convenience. Motor vehicles, consumer durables, office equipment, etc., are commonly traded-in as soon as they begin to show wear and tear. Yet, as wartime experiences proved, the useful working lifetimes of such goods are not strictly limited; they depend on the skills and attention of maintenance staffs and upon the patience of the user. For example, if it were socially acceptable, a quick way for a free enterprise country to increase the working lives of its motor vehicles would be simply to increase the tax on new ones and decrease that on old ones. Market forces would then bring about the required result, through a great flourishing of service garages.

Conclusion

As with energy, Man can have all the materials he wants, at a price. Indeed, the position for materials is on the whole easier than that for energy, although it is also more complex. It is easier because matter is never destroyed (except in nuclear transformations) but merely re-arranged, so that used materials can in principle be recovered and recycled; also, because it is the properties of materials that are usually wanted, not the particular substances themselves, so that a large measure of substitution of one material for another is possible; furthermore, by the expenditure of additional energy on extractive processes, extremely large low-grade sources of materials could be tapped; and, finally, there is a wide range of almost inexhaustible materials, such as iron, aluminium, magnesium, silicon, cement, glass and wood. The materials problem is complex because many kinds of properties are wanted and a great variety of materials is necessary to provide them. The resource and economic positions are different for each one. Some, although not those used in bulk, could become critically short in the near future; for example, mercury, tin, and perhaps phosphate. Although vital, they are nevertheless small components of the world's material requirements and so their price could rise considerably, thus enabling lower-grade sources to be worked, without greatly increasing the world's total expenditure on materials.

But all such adjustments take time, especially where new technologies have to be developed and applied. Economists tend to forget this when they speak of 'leaving it to the market to sort out problems of scarcity'. There is indeed a variety of responses open for dealing with the challenge of materials shortages but many of them rest on the assumption that more energy will be available for extractive processes, in future, whereas the reverse is a likely possibility. Thermodynamically, the processes of extracting and concentrating materials from dilute sources are extremely inefficient and therefore costly, partly because a great deal of energy is wasted in crushing up rock and partly because, even when the molecules concerned are dissolved in water it is difficult to get hold of them without scouring through vast amounts of liquid. It seems likely that energy will increasingly become the main determining factor in the supply of materials and hence that, so far as materials are concerned, an energy—cost theory of value will have some validity.

4 Food

The World of Agriculture

Over half of the people in the world support themselves by farming. In the less developed countries, where the typical family has little choice but to grow its own food, the proportion may approach 100%. In the more industrialized countries, where technical advances have enabled one farmer to feed many people, the proportion is much lower. At the present state of agricultural technology, the lowest limit is about 7%. This is attained in the USA, which is self-sufficient in agricultural production. In Britain, which also has a highly productive agricultural industry, less than 4% of the population is engaged in farming, but Britain imports nearly half of its food.

The amount of the world's land surface used for arable farming is only about 11%. This may seem small and suggest that Man has plenty of reserve land to call upon, when needed, but in fact only about 25% of the world's land is suitable for agriculture. The rest is too frozen, mountainous, arid, or wet. In Asia and Europe, where the population densities are high, over 90% of the possible agricultural land is already in use. For example, the arable land per person (in hectares*) is only 0.06 in Japan, 0.07 in Holland, 0.13 in China; but 0.6 in Africa, 0.82 in North America, 0.94 in the USSR and 2.32 in Oceania; and the world average is 0.39. [Source: UN Food and Agricultural Organisation, Production Yearbook.]

In terms of energy content, cereal crops provide just over one-half of the world's food (of which wheat and rice each provide about one-fifth). Animal products, root crops, fruits and vegetables, and fats and oils, each provide about one-tenth; and the remaining tenth is contributed by sugar, fish and minor products. The yields of crops differ greatly in various parts of the world. In countries with advanced agricultural systems, cereal yields of 4 to 5 tons per hectare are obtained, whereas in the less developed but agriculturally important countries they are more commonly about 0.5 to 1.5 tons per hectare. The world average of grain yields is about 1.7 tons per hectare. On the basis of an energy content in grain of about 4 million Calories† per ton, of 1.7 tons per hectare, and of 0.39 hectares per person,

---

* 1 hectare = 10 000 sq. metres = 2.47 acres.
† The Calorie is the standard unit of food energy;
  1 Calorie = 1 kilocalorie = 0.00116 kilowatt-hours = 4190 joules.

the total world food production is in principle about 2.6 million Calories per person annually, i.e. about 7000 Calories per day. This is well above a person's daily requirement of energy food (about 2500 Calories), but because of food losses and for other reasons only a fraction of the potential crop is available in practice.

The style of farming varies enormously from place to place, of course, not only for obvious geographical and climatic reasons, but also because of the great differences in economic activity, population density and political structure in various parts of the world. At one extreme is the *subsistence farmer* in a poor country, just about able to grow enough to feed himself and his own family, on a plot of about 2 hectares, and with almost nothing to sell as a *cash crop* in the market. At the other extreme is the large and highly mechanized farm, run as an *industrial business* entirely for cash crops, and on which there may be only one farm worker for 100 hectares. But most farms in the world are individual *family farms*, i.e. in which one farmer and his family supply most of the labour to run their farm. The family farm provides a traditional, natural and much cherished way of life for mankind, but it often has difficulty in remaining efficient and competitive because of sub-division of the land into unduly small plots, amongst the growing members of a family, and because of lack of financial resources to invest in farm machinery, buildings, fertilizers, etc. A large business farm, provided that the controlling organization is intelligent enough to run it successfully, can often be more efficient and productive than a family farm. This has led to the formation of *cooperative farms*, of which very successful examples are the Israeli *kibbutzim* in which a group of families owns and works a large estate and its farm equipment. The *collective farms* of the USSR, on the other hand, are owned by the State, which lays down the controlling policies in central State 5-year plans.

Economics of Agriculture

There are two outstanding economic features of the farming industry. First, farm workers usually have lower incomes than average. This is to some extent because they are often less well-placed than townspeople to switch into more highly paid kinds of work. But it is also because most countries have a surplus of farm workers, as a result of agricultural mechanization in advanced countries, or of an over-grown rural population on a limited land area in many poor countries. The marginal productivity of farm labour, which determines the economic income level, has thus tended towards zero due to this surplus.

The second feature is that the prices of agricultural products often fluctuate wildly. For example, from January 1972 to April 1974 the price of Bangkok rice shot up from $131 to $630 a ton, i.e. by 380%; similarly, the export price of US hard winter wheat climbed from $60 a ton in early

1972 up to $220 in early 1974 and then dropped half-way back again a few months later. The general reason for such price fluctuations is the unstable relation between supply and demand for foodstuffs. Supply is naturally variable, partly for seasonal reasons and partly due to factors such as the weather, outside the farmers' control, so that at some times there are surplusses, at others shortages. Demand, on the other hand, is fairly constant and *inelastic to price*, at least within a single growing season, since the average person is satisfied to eat at all times his normal amount of food. As people become wealthier, they generally spend a smaller part of their money on food. Of course, eating habits do change with affluence and some of the more expensive foods (e.g. meat) absorb a lot of food in their production, but such habits generally change less rapidly and drastically than the season-to-season fluctuations in farm outputs. In any case the main *income elasticity* of demand is for *food services*, e.g. restaurant meals and convenience foods, rather than for basic food as such.

This problem of economic instability in the agricultural industry has been of great concern to governments, who have at times introduced drastic corrective measures. In an attempt to stop the fall of coffee prices, Brazil burned about 4 million tons of surplus stocks in the 1930s. Similarly, the USA in the 1960s paid farmers to reduce their acreages of crops and to leave some of their land idle, as a *Soil Bank*.

While seasonal fluctuations can to some extent be overcome by the practice of building up *buffer stocks*, the more difficult challenges for governments are those to do with general productivity. In much of the world, as we shall discuss later, low agricultural productivity is the great problem. But in the economically developed countries the opposite is more usually true. Because of rapidly rising productivity, against a fairly fixed demand, the tendency in these countries is towards surplusses and redundant farm labour. For example, the USA Soil Bank policy was partly frustrated because the rising productivity of the remaining used land to some extent made up for that left idle.

Governments in the developed countries have tried many ways of maintaining farm prices and incomes, sometimes through *import controls* against cheap overseas food, but more generally through *support policies* commonly based on *guaranteed prices*. The method in Britain until recently was through *deficiency payments* in which, when a farmer's average realized prices fell below a guaranteed level, the government paid him the difference. In the USA, and now in the EEC with its common agricultural policy (CAP), the authorities promise to buy all produce at a certain *intervention price*, which they can then store or export at subsidized and sometimes bargain prices.

An obvious effect of this governmental intervention in the transactions of an otherwise free market economy is that a favourable guaranteed price encourages over-production and the accumulation of mountainous quantities of the product. A more general problem, common to all attempts to steer a country's agriculture by central State policies, is that because farms differ in their circumstances — size, soil, climate, local markets, etc. — a standardized intervention price that allows one farm to flourish may ruin another.

Land as a Scarce Resource

The most obvious fact about land as an economic resource is that the world's land area is virtually fixed. However, the depth and quality of its topsoil is variable. Moreover, some agricultural land is lost each year to other purposes. In Britain, for example, some 20 000 hectares (slightly over 0.1% of its agricultural land) are taken out of agricultural production each year, for housing, roads, etc.; developments which often take place on flat, well-drained, and accessible land that is also good for agriculture. Furthermore, food production has to compete for land against other uses, e.g. forests and non-food crops, open-cast mining, national parks and recreational land; although of course geographical factors often leave only one of these alternatives as a sensible use of the land in a given locality.

Regarding land, then, as a scarce resource, is it in any sense being 'used up' by agriculture? Of course, agriculture, particularly the modern intensive kind, has *external diseconomies*, for example through the discharge of excess chemical fertilizers and animal wastes into rivers, etc., and the clearing of hedgerows, copses, etc., which destroys amenity and habitats for wild life. Such life may also be destroyed more directly by agricultural insecticides. But what about the effects on the agricultural land itself? These can also be destructive. Clearing the natural vegetation may leave the topsoil exposed to *erosion* by wind and water; in many parts of the world farming and grazing are causing topsoil to be removed faster than it is formed. Soil erosion, which turned much of North Africa from a fertile region to a desert and which led to the 'dust bowls' of the USA in the 1930s, is today destroying millions of hectares of agricultural land in various parts of the world. By natural processes, topsoil can be replaced only very gradually, needing several centuries to create a one inch depth. Soil erosion is, moreover, not the only problem. One other is that excessive water pumping, for agricultural irrigation, can alter the water table and so make the soil waterlogged or salty. Again, heavy farm machinery can beat a clay soil down into an impermeable and infertile compacted mass.

Such considerations have led some economists to doubt the common view that a well-cultivated farm could continue indefinitely yielding its same constant crop. The fact however is, both in theory and practice, that the productivity of agricultural land need *not* be exhaustible. The only truly irreversible process which occurs is the degradation of energy from high-quality to low-quality form (with some high-quality sunlight captured by photosynthesis and preserved in biological organisms) and this is basically the same on a cultivated farm as on wild prairie or primeval forest. All other changes consist of redistributions of matter, which are not in themselves irreversible. In practice, it is well-known that by good husbandry the agricultural qualities of a soil can be not only maintained but even improved. Many European farmlands have been worked hard for centuries, yet their soil is in better condition today and more productive than ever. We ought then only to regard agricultural land as a *consumable* resource in those cases where it is used unintelligently or negligently; with good farming practice, it can be preserved and improved, although the cost of taking care of it should of course be included in the costs of production.

As we saw in Chapter 1, land which is made freely available for all may get ruined by over-use and neglect. It was this problem that led many years ago to the introduction of the system of *land enclosures* in which the wasteful communal open-field gave way to the enclosure, by hedges and fences, of smaller fields whose cultivation and stocking could be controlled by their individual owners. In this way enclosed farmland acquired a *price* value, based on the return it was able to earn, and the individual farmer was thus given an incentive to improve the quality of the land, *his* land — for example, by drainage, crop-rotation, manuring, wind-breaks — without fear that his efforts would be wasted by the depredations of wandering herds. The earning capacities of some soils quickly rose as much as tenfold by such improvements. These economic changes occurred two centuries ago, but we see a similar development today in the world's *fisheries*. The seas have traditionally been 'open commons' for everyone and, as such, have in places been almost fished out, so that many countries today are trying to 'enclose' more of their offshore waters by legislation aimed at making it 'illegal' for others to fish there.

It was the consideration of the earning power of farm land that led David Ricardo (1817) to his theory of economic value. As population increased, he argued, increasingly poor quality land had to be brought into use to feed the additional mouths. Such land would give less return for the money and effort put into it. This process would continue until the only remaining unused land was so poor as to be not worth bringing into cultivation. Clearly, the economic value of this *marginal land*, for agriculture, is zero under the economic conditions prevailing at the time. However, Ricardo said, *costs* and *profits* tend to be the same on *all* land, whether marginal or not, because labour costs are the same, wherever applied, and because if profits on the good land were to climb high, extra capital investment would flood in there until, by the *law of diminishing returns*, the profits earned by this extra investment in farming the good land fell to the general level of profits elsewhere. But a hectare of good land would nevertheless be earning a higher *return* than one of poor land. Since this extra return cannot be attributed to costs and profits it represents a true value of the good land, for the use of which an economic *rent* could thus be charged.

Food versus Fuel

Is modern, intensive, food production using up the earth's capital resources? In some cases this is certainly true. Cattle farms can raise larger
herds than their own land can feed, by importing animal foodstuffs. In
a modern chicken battery about six times as much energy is fed in as
is delivered in the eggs produced. A large amount of energy is used in the
production of nitrogen fertilizer, which is essential to most modern farming; and the desalination of water, for farming in dry countries, is also
costly in energy.

   The resource most generally imported into modern farming is in fact
energy. About one-third of the energy contained in the USA corn crop has,
indirectly, been supplied from fuel. For the British grain crop the corresponding figure is about one-half. For dairy products it is much greater
than unity. There are several ways of looking at these figures. First, the
fact that it is profitable to convert energy so inefficiently to meat, milk,
eggs, etc. reflects the value which Society sets on having this energy in the
form of food, especially protein, rather than as fuel. Second, in the production of grain, more energy is delivered than is consumed from fuel, so that
the bargain is a good one. Even before we begin to count the merits of
grain as a *food*, we have in modern arable farming a system for amplifying
the earth's stock of carbonaceous fuel, by a factor of two or three in the
throughput. In this sense, such farming is a very effective *solar energy*
industry, even though we prefer to use its product as food rather than
fuel. If, hypothetically, the input fuel energy were provided by using
some of last season's crop as fuel, such an agricultural system could
be completely self-sufficient and so could be kept going indefinitely.
However, the choice of Society today is to prefer food to fuel; and
because of this, modern intensive arable farming, through no fault of its
own, is providing yet another channel for the consumption of the earth's
stock of fuel resources.

   The price of energy in the form of food such as grain is generally some
3 to 5 times its price as fuel such as oil; its price in the form of meat and
animal products is several times higher still. These figures show the value
that Society places on food (for body-building as well as for metabolic
energy) rather than fuel. However, the economic balance might just about
be favourable for growing fuel crops, as in the old days of the charcoal
forest, on land where there is less opportunity or need for food growing.
Photosynthesis not only captures solar energy; it also fixes carbon from
the air. To meet future needs for premium hydrocarbon fuels, e.g. for
air transport, the growth of vegetation might become economically attractive.

   The two most interesting possibilities are sugar production in the
tropics and softwood forestry in temperate zones. It seems likely that
industrial alcohol fuel could be produced at below $1 per gallon, by

growing sugarcane and then converting it by fermentation, which is marginally economic for premium engine fuel. The possibilities for fuel from forest wood are similar. However, the land area taken up in providing a major fuel supply would have to be very large. For example, over half of Britain would need to be forested to supply its present petroleum and gas requirements. The other possibility is to make fuel from organic waste products, the total amount of which is probably sufficient to supply about one-tenth of energy needs, although the costs of collecting and processing usually make this uneconomic under present conditions.

The Problem of Feeding the World

Are there limits to the number of people that the world can feed? If so, what determines these limits and how near to them are we? As with energy and materials, the theoretical food limits are very high but the practical ones fall much lower. Modern estimates have confirmed what Leibig said in 1862; i.e. that the world's land can product about 100 billion tons (dry weight) of organic matter a year. On the other hand, the old optimism about the seas as 'limitless sources of food' has faded with the discovery that the oceans beyond the continental shelf are inherently barren; the world's seas are now thought able to provide only 50 billion tons (dry weight) a year.

These land and sea totals thus amount to about 40 tons per person per year at the present level of world population (about 4 billion), which is some 100 times what is needed. But this is of course a totally unrealistic figure, for Man is unable to 'run' the earth biologically at more than a minute fraction of its theoretical efficiency. There is encouragement in this since it means that we are not yet up against fundamental limits and have a reasonable basis on which to hope that we may be able in future to improve our present low efficiency. Of course, modern agriculture is eating up natural resources; even where the quality of agricultural land is being maintained, high-quality energy is being consumed in agriculture. But we have also noted that this consumption is a social decision, not an agricultural imperative, since most farming provides more energy than it consumes.

Malthus based his view on the inevitable ultimate effects of continuing population growth. He argued that a critical population density must eventually be reached, beyond which there would be too many people to feed from a given land area under a given agricultural system. In practice, of course, agricultural systems are not static because technical improvements are constantly taking place, particularly recently with the development of high-yielding strains of wheat and rice, in the so-called 'Green Revolution'. Nevertheless there is much evidence of the Malthusian limit being reached in past civilizations. Even in this century famines have so far killed possibly 20 million people. Today there are several parts of the world where the Malthusian limits are now reached or exceeded. Such countries keep going, despite their insufficient food production, either by a mixture of international food assistance and semi-starvation; or if they are more fortunate, as in Britain and Japan, by trading manufactured goods and services for imported food and raw materials.

In the developed countries, taken as a whole, food production in recent years has been increasing at about 2.9% a year; and population at only 1.1% a year, so leaving a 1.8% yearly increase in food per person. Since personal consumption is fairly constant (apart from effects of changes in habits, such as eating more meat) the problem for these highly productive countries is one of controlling production so as to supply domestic needs and some exports, but to avoid unsaleable surplusses that could ruin their farmers. But this is of course a trifling problem compared with the gigantic one, facing the developing countries, of feeding their peoples (see Fig. 4.1). These countries have expanded their food production at

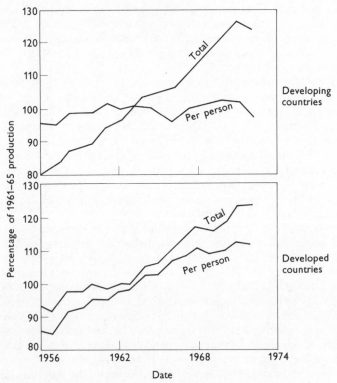

Fig. 4.1 Growth of food production, total and per person, in developing and developed countries (based on US Department of Agriculture figures).

about the same rate as the developed ones, but their populations have been growing too fast to leave any significant increase in food per person. As a result, the present position is that two-thirds of the world's peoples are continually underfed. In energy content the average shortfall is about 6% but becomes much more severe in bad growing seasons.

The development of world trade in food also reflects the same problem, as shown in Table 4.1.

Table 4.1 Changing Patterns in the Grain Trade

(+ = net exports; − = net imports; in millions of tons)

	1934–38	1948–52	1960	1966	1973
North America	+5	+23	+39	+59	+91
Australia, New Zealand	+3	+3	+6	+8	+6
W. Europe	−24	−22	−25	−27	−19
Africa	+1	0	−2	−7	−5
Latin America	+9	+1	0	+5	−3
USSR, E. Europe	+5	not known	0	−4	−27
Asia	+2	−6	−17	−34	−43

(Figures based on US Department of Agriculture data)

We see that exports from North America (and on a smaller scale, Australia and New Zealand) have grown tremendously, so that these countries are becoming the world's granaries. The other great trend, depressing in the case of Asia and disturbing in that of the USSR and East Europe, is the growing inability of these regions to feed themselves.

In 1962 the developing countries had to spend $3000 m on imported food. On the basis of the present trends, the corresponding figure in 1985 could rise (even at 1962 prices) to an impossible $40 000 m, for by then they may need over twice as much food as they did in 1962.

Whether the 'granary' countries will still have the capacity to supply the consumer countries, when the gap has grown still larger, is doubtful. Some alleviation would be possible if people in the well-fed parts of the world reduced the meat content of their diets (which is unnecessarily high), because cattle as food-converters consume about ten times as much food as they produce. But this could only be a subsidiary measure. A major problem is that many of the developing countries are too poor to be able either to buy imported food, in the required amounts, or to invest in all the things — fertilizers, water supply and drainage, farm machinery, fuel to run it, pesticides, weed killers, storage and transport facilities, roads and market facilities — that are needed to modernize their agriculture and to lift its productivity to the levels attained in developed countries.

While emergency shortages in bad growing years can only be dealt with by providing the affected countries with food as a form of international aid — and the accumulation of a world grain store of about 100 m tons would greatly help to buffer the effects of lean years — the long-term solution must be to help the developing countries by means of finance (as well as technical assistance) to strengthen their agricultural systems to the required level, as well as to encourage their efforts to reduce population growth. The bare minimum of financial assistance needed for agriculture is of order $5000 m a year; this may seem large, but it is nevertheless only about one-third of the value, at commercial prices, of the grain traded across world markets today; and less than one-tenth of the balance-of-payments surplusses now accruing annually to the oil-exporting countries.

Conclusion

It is at first sight surprising that highly industrialized countries are, in general, also the most efficient at food production, but this mainly reflects the fact that, notwithstanding its dependence on weather and the inelasticity of demand for its products, farming is as responsive to the techniques of industrial productivity as any manufacturing process. Indeed, the main technical trend in modern agriculture has been *mechanization*, the replacement of both animal and human effort by that of fuel-driven machines. Although most farming is still a solar-energy industry, which delivers more energy in food than it takes in fuel, the fact that Society is now using the industry increasingly to convert fuel into food is dangerous, in view of the fact that the world may soon be running short simultaneously of *both* food and fuel.

As with energy and materials, the gap between the high theoretical limits of world food production and the low practical limits is very wide. Agricultural research can of course help to narrow it, as for example in the development of high-yielding crops, but it takes time. The main constraint, however, is the lack of capital to improve agricultural efficiency in the developing countries. This is needed today in very large amounts and will increase sharply with the growth in world populations. Even if the capital were available there is very little time now to bring in all the large-scale changes that will be needed, as the world moves towards an era of famine at the end of this century.

5 The Natural Environment

Pollution

We have seen that energy is conserved but its *quality* is not; and it is its quality, not the energy as such, that commands a price, since it is a scarce resource which we value but consume. On an increasingly crowded planet the same argument is beginning to apply to those resources such as air, water and space, which we have traditionally been able to regard as abundant free gifts of nature. For they, like energy, have *quality* — the cleanliness and freshness of air, purity of water, greenness of landscape, quietness of surroundings — which we value and which in the more densely occupied parts of the world is becoming scarce. And, again like energy, it is the quality of these environmental resources that we consume.

Pollution is usually regarded as the release, into a shared environment and against the common interest, of an offensive by-product or waste; but from the economic standpoint there are advantages in following the analogy with quality of energy by regarding pollution as the *consumption of environmental quality*. For example, a smoky fire consumes clean air and replaces it with soot-laden air. The advantage of looking at pollution this way is that environmental quality can then be considered as an *input*, to any economic activity, on exactly the same basis as the other inputs such as labour, capital, and raw materials. In the words of W. Beckerman (*Pricing for Pollution*, The Institute of Economic Affairs, 1975) 'pollution is objectionable because it constitutes the "using up" of a resource to which we attach value, such as clean air, or water, or peace and quiet . . .. If we could always provide ourselves with *unlimited* amounts of clean air or water we would not mind how much of it was "used up" by the polluter . . .. The key point is that the environment is a scarce resource and pollution is, in effect, a use of this resource.'

Pollution has of course been a townsman's problem for centuries. In 1273 an edict was issued in London prohibiting the use of coal as being 'prejudicial to health'. In the mid-19th century it was unbearable to breathe in the House of Commons unless the window curtains had been soaked in chloride of lime, because of the sickening stench from the polluted Thames. And in the great London smog of 1952 there were 4000 extra deaths, attributed to smoke and sulphurous fumes. But with Man now making such a big impact on the natural world — for example, having changed the face of much of the land and now mining several minerals at rates greater than those of global geological attrition – pollution has also become a countryman's problem through the discharge on to the land, waters and air, of waste pesticides, fertilizers, animal effluents, and mining and industrial debris. It could even become a global problem, due to the emission of carbon dioxide, nitrous oxides, smoke, waste heat, nuclear materials, DDT, and aerosol chemicals, into the atmosphere. That the global environment has only a limited ability to absorb the effects of a major assault upon it was shown by the Krakatoa volcanic eruption in 1883, the dust clouds from which caused the average temperature in the USA to drop by a few degrees during the following year, giving widespread crop failures.

Modern agricultural and manufacturing industries have become highly productive and efficient by consuming environmental resources on a far greater scale than ever before. But this same high productivity creates additional economic resources that can, of Society so wishes, be used to protect and improve the environment. It is a problem for the future, which of these two opposing trends will win – either the consumption of environmental quality by agriculture and industry, or the preservation of quality by environmental improvement programmes through the application of the additional resources being created by modern technology and economic activity. Up till now, the economic resources for environmental improvement have usually been found when urgently required, but have rarely been satisfactorily provided except under dire threat of an environmental disaster. The general position today is patchy; for example, some parts of the Mediterranean are becoming highly polluted, whereas the Thames in London has recently become a fishable river; clean air acts have eliminated smog from many cities, including London, but acid-bearing rain is affecting the forests and fishing rivers of Scandinavia.

Man's Impact on the Environment

We live at a time when mankind's impact on the natural environment has reached an unprecedented intensity and when there is great and growing anxiety about the earth's physical and biological capacity to continue to carry such a burden. The world's population in recent decades has been growing at over 2% a year, which means that a 70-year old person now lives in a world *four* times as crowded as when he or she was born. The change in turnover of natural resources – both on the input side, which involves the depletion of non-renewable stocks, and on the output side, which involves the creation of waste products – has been even more drastic, due to the combined effects of population and economic growth. Our 70-year old has thus lived through an era of *tenfold* increase in industrial production, in consumption of natural resources and in creation of waste and pollution.

Although the rates of turnover may change, there can be no doubt that

Man's impact on the environment will continue to increase in the foreseeable future. For, quite apart from the effects of rising industrial and agricultural productivity, there is the simple fact that most of the future parents of 20 years time are already with us and are an unprecedentedly large fraction of the world's population. There is an inevitable delay between a change in the rate of human reproduction and its effect on the growth of population. For instance, even if it were possible for the world's peoples to confine themselves, from now onwards, to a *net reproduction rate* of only two children per couple, the world's population would still go on growing for another 60 years or so, before levelling off (at a value about 50% above the present 4000 million). It follows that in a realistic discussion about Man's impact on the environment, in the foreseeable future, we have to think in terms of world populations well above the present level.

Most of these people will live in cities, of a size, complexity and density, that even by today's standards will be breathtaking. The pattern for the future is to be found in the miles of urbanization in the eastern USA or north-west Europe; in the overcrowding of Hong Kong; in the huge apartment blocks of Moscow, Paris and Rome; and above all in the squalor of many cities such as, for example, Calcutta, Bogota and Kinshasa. The world already has cities containing 10 million inhabitants each, Tokyo is expected soon to have 25 million, and in the not too distant future the city of 100 million is a likely possibility.

Man, as a living creature, cannot avoid creating some pollutants, i.e. body wastes, stale breaths and products of bodily decay, the amounts of which rise in proportion to the population. These basic pollutants, as also those waste products from unindustrialized agriculture, are natural substances which can generally be disposed of fairly readily by the earth's natural population of bacteria, but in crowded human communities, in industrial societies and intensive farms, the densities and character of the pollutants raise more difficult problems and their satisfactory treatment and disposal becomes increasingly expensive.

In Britain, for example, where each person generates on average about 40 gallons daily of water-borne waste, recent expenditure on sewerage schemes alone has amounted to about £250 million annually. Furthermore, it has been estimated that Britain's needs for fresh water are growing at over 2% a year. Most of this extra water will have to come from the rivers, and it will go back to them as effluent. But the carrying capacity of the rivers, for such a burden, will not increase, so that if the quality of river water is to be held at only the present level, it will be necessary to purify the effluent more than at present, to compensate for its additional volume. However, the cost of effluent treatment rises sharply with the attempt to remove the last 5% or 1% of impurity, so that the costs of pollution control in future must escalate, except insofar as they can be offset by new and improved technological processes of waste treatment.

Environmental Costs

Since consumption of environmental quality is a fundamental condition of life itself, pollution costs can never be wholly avoided under conditions where environmental quality is a scarce resource, although Society can at least in principle choose how large they shall be (by regulating the level and nature of its activities), in what form they shall be paid, and upon whom the burden of paying them shall fall. The traditional position, based on the old assumption that the environment is 'infinite' and free for all, which is no longer valid in crowded societies, has been for the polluter not to pay the cost of his consumption of environmental quality, in which case pollution is an *external cost* of his activities, i.e. an *external diseconomy* borne by some or all of his general community.

Environmental costs can take various forms which have been described by the *US Council on Environmental Quality* as *damage costs, avoidance costs, transaction costs* and *abatement costs*. Damage costs are the direct costs of the pollution itself, e.g. the cost of bronchitis, etc. in people afflicted by smog, or the cost of fish losses due to poisonous effluent discharged into a river. Avoidance costs are those incurred by people in attempting to separate themselves from pollution, e.g. the cost of sound-proofing a home to keep out the noise of aircraft or traffic. Both damage and avoidance costs are external costs and they can be large. For example, it was estimated in 1972 that costs to local inhabitants of house value losses, near London Airport, and of moving away from there, came to about £60 m a year. Transaction costs are the costs of gathering information about pollution, especially by monitoring, and of preparing and administering anti-pollution policies. Abatement costs, which usually dominate discussions of pollution economics, are those incurred in preventing or abating pollution, e.g. the cost of a sewage treatment plant.

There is a roughly inverse relation between damage and avoidance costs, on the one hand, and transaction and abatement costs, on the other. Where the latter are not charged, the former will run high, and vice versa. Somewhere between lies the optimum. The best return to Society is not gained by trying to 'stop all pollution'. Indeed this is impossible. Chasing the *last few* atoms of mercury in edible fish, or of lead in city air, would cost an inordinate amount of money, which might have been put to other more beneficial uses. In a best use of resources, some pollution has to be accepted. Nor does the optimum necessarily lie anywhere near the point where expenditure on abatement is equal to the unabated external costs.

The principle which determines the optimum is the *marginality principle*, mentioned in Chapter 1, of which costs are one aspect, benefits another. According to this, the economic resources of Society are deployed to the greatest benefit when each particular economic activity — which in this case might be the monitoring and abatement of pollution — is pushed to that level at which the cost of providing one more unit of it, i.e. its *marginal unit cost*, is just equal to the value, or *price*, of benefit which that unit confers. For, if we go beyond this point the costs are too much, for the further benefit received, in which case Society is better served by withdrawing some resources from that activity and spending them on something else; and if we do not go far enough, there is then on average a better return to be had by adding resources to this effort rather than elsewhere in the economy. The optimum point is thus determined by the equality of *increments* of cost and benefit, which may be quite different from the points where abatement costs equal external costs, or where pollution is 'stopped altogether'.

The difficulty in practice with this theory is that the costs and benefits are generally not easily measurable or even quantitatively definable. What is it worth, to see trees in blossom? Thus, in practice, expenditure on pollution abatement has to be determined largely by intuitive judgements. Of course, where a serious emergency is caused, as for example with the London killer smog of 1952 or the Japanese deaths by mercury poisoning at Minamata Bay in 1956, action to combat the pollution becomes imperative. But in less extreme cases it is usually a matter of judgement on social priorities whether to go on putting up with an existing unsatisfactory level of environmental quality or to spend an increased effort on improving it at the expense of foregoing opportunities to do other desirable things.

Pollution costs are generally estimated nationally to be of the order of 1% of GNP. The percentages given for some OECD countries over the period 1971–75 were 1.6 (USA), 1.8 (W. Germany), 0.6 (Italy) and 0.5 (Netherlands) (OECD Report, *Collection and Analysis of Pollution Control Cost Data*, Environmental Report, 4 March 1972). This OECD Report concluded that pollution 'costs during the first half of this decade will have only a relatively modest effect on the ability of a nation to satisfy any other urgent needs of a society'. Other estimates lead to similar conclusions. Thus the World Bank (*Report on The Limits to Growth*, September 1972) has given figures which show that 80–90% of present pollution can be removed at relatively low cost and that, in the USA, a substantial increase in the abatement of air, water, and solid waste pollution could be achieved by the expenditure of $40–50 billion a year, which might amount to about 1.2% of GNP in the year 2000.

Making the Polluter Pay

Pollution is of interest to economists because it provides, through its external diseconomies, another example of where the general public interest is something different from the mere sum of the private interests of its individuals. Like *Keynes' General Theory*, the economics of pollution deals with problems which, although conceptually much simpler than those of employment, interest and money, nevertheless contain an essential *social* feature.

In those communities where environmental quality has become a scarce resource but is erroneously still treated as if it were free – and for global pollution this means the world community – the costs of pollution are usually not borne by those responsible for it. An overall effect of this is that the economic resources of Society are, on this basis, not deployed to the greatest overall benefit. The social optimum point, where social marginal costs equal prices, is not located and those activities which cause pollution are pushed too far. The reason is that when the polluters – who may be private individuals, firms, public authorities, or even entire

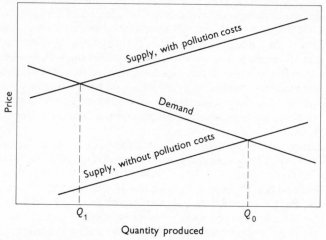

Fig. 5.1   If producers and consumers ignore the pollution costs in a production, market equilibrium is reached when the quantity produced is Q_0. This exceeds the socially optimal amount of the quantity produced, Q_1, which takes account of the pollution costs.

countries – do not bear the total costs of their activities, because their pollution costs are exported to others, they seek an optimum activity on the basis of only their own *private* costs, which are smaller than the social costs; and the balance point, where marginal costs equal prices, in this case then lies farther over, in favour of more of the activity in question (see Fig. 5.1). In this way the community ends up with a macro-economically unbalanced deployment of its resources and it thereby fails to gain the fullest benefit from them. A holiday town, for example, might suffer more from lost tourist trade than it gains from additional industries attracted to it by low municipal rates which charge insufficiently for keeping the place clean and attractive. When only private costs, not full social costs, are taken into account, pollution abatement also often gets neglected. The upstream town finds it cheaper to let the local river wash its sewage away, rather than build a sewage treatment works, even though someone else, downstream, then has to suffer a dirty river.

Goods are desirable and carry prices, i.e. are exchanged for positive money. Pollution is undesirable and should therefore have a *negative* price, i.e. be exchanged for *negative* money. But an exchange for negative money is merely a back-to-front way of saying that an outflow of positive money should accompany an outflow of pollution; in other words that a polluter should pay a tax in proportion to the amount of pollution he delivers to the community. This is the basic economic argument that the *polluter should pay* for his pollution, by a *tax*, as advocated for example by W. Beckerman (in *Pricing for Pollution*, The Institute of Economic Affairs, 1975). If his tax is set equal to the cost to the community of having the pollution inflicted upon it, then the polluter will bear financially the full cost of his pollution and will thus be encouraged to seek, in his own best interests, that balance of activities at which the marginal social costs equal prices, which is also the point of optimum social benefit. In this way, the price mechanism of the free market economy can play its part in finding the socially most rewarding way of dealing with pollution problems, as it can with other problems of scarce resources; and in effect it does it by regarding environmental *quality* in the normal economic way as a scarce resource, to be charged for in accordance with the amount consumed, through a pollution tax.

Despite the compelling logic of its economic argument, the pollution tax has generally been less preferred than *regulatory controls* on amounts of pollution allowed to be emitted. Of course, where the social damage is sufficiently grave, it may be necessary flatly to forbid the activity. Few of us would be happy about trying to prevent murder by placing a tax on it (J. E. Meade, *Economic Policy and the Threat of Doom*, The Galton Lecture 1972). But in less extreme cases taxing will be more efficient economically than regulation, because people's circumstances differ and the social optimum cannot be found if they are all forced into the same Procrustean bed of a standard regulation size. Moreover, a tax leaves the individual with freedom and incentive to search for new and cheaper way to reduce his pollution.

Conclusion

All living processes, including Man's economic activities, consume environmental *quality*, just as they consume the quality of energy. On today's crowded planet the quality of the environment, unlike that of mercy, is strained. Environmental quality is becoming a scarce and valued resource, which should therefore command a *price*. This price should be paid by its consumers in proportion to the amount consumed, as a *pollution tax*, set at the level which will bring the optimum point of each consumer's private interest to the same position as the social optimum point, where the social marginal costs and prices are equal. Society will in this way be led to deploy its various economic resources in the most generally beneficial way. In practice, problems of measurement and of lack of quantitative information make it difficult to control pollution on the basis of a full cost—benefit analysis, and allocations of resources to the abatement of pollution have usually to be decided by empirical judgements of the social interest. Present experience suggests that pollution can be held down to generally acceptable levels, by today's standards in industrial countries, through the expenditure of about 1 to 2% of GNP on controls and abatement.

6 The Next Fifty Years

Limits to Growth

The space pictures of the Earth remind us vividly that we live on a *finite* ball. What is its *capacity* to support Man and his works; and at what populations and material standards of living? Many people have now revived these old Malthusian questions, most notably J. W. Forrester (*World Dynamics*, Wright-Allen Press, Inc., 1971) and D. H. Meadows, et al. (*The Limits to Growth*, Universe Books, New York, 1972). A great debate has raged over them; usually (but with exceptions both ways) the *environmentalists* have taken a pessimistic view — based on the galloping increases in population and turnover of natural resources — and the *economists* have taken an optimistic one — based on the ability of free market economies to cushion the effects of impending shortages, through the responses of producers and consumers to the various incentives and disincentives of rising prices.

Environmentalists tend to overlook the economic factors, especially the power of market forces to stimulate Man's ingenuity and inventiveness in solving problems of shortages. In 17th century England the inability of the forests to meet anticipated needs for iron-making charcoal and for ships' timbers raised alarms, but wood gave way to coke in 18th century furnaces and to iron in the 19th century ships. More recently, the world's supply of nitrogen fertilizer, from natural sources, looked precarious at the beginning of this century, until Haber discovered how to fix nitrogen from air, in synthetic ammonia.

For their part, economists tend to underestimate the difficulties in responding quickly to a change in market forces. It is often said, about shortages, 'leave it to the market forces to take care of them; the pattern of supply and demand will always provoke the necessary counter-measures'. So it will, in the long run; but, as Keynes remarked, in the long run we are dead. The present high price of oil opens up a fine commercial opportunity to bring alternatives and substitutes into being. Many people are no doubt striving hard to do just this, but it cannot happen overnight; not even less in than five to ten years. True, market forces can also provoke various short-term measures; but these are generally of a more brutal kind. It is hard to tell a starving man that he is correctly obeying the economist's principle that, when a resource becomes scarce, its price goes up and its use goes down.

There is, moreover, a new factor to be taken into account. The pace of world economic growth has never gone faster than now. Since the second World War, the turnover of natural resources has been doubling every 15 to 20 years. At this rate, a finite resource could be more than half untouched today (1976), yet still be all gone well before the end of the century. This leaves very little time indeed for the research, development and industrialization necessary to adjust to future shortages, certainly much less than the time now usually required for the maturing of large new industries such as nuclear power, solar energy, sea-bed mining, and fish farming.

Returning to the question of the finite earth it is clear that, taking the world as a whole, Man is not yet anywhere near its physical limits. The environment could be kept generally clean and sweet by the expenditure of not more than about 2% GWP (= Gross World Product) on anti-pollution measures. The earth's natural resources are very large, compared with Man's consumption, and any shortages we at present suffer come mainly from our technological and economic limitations. Energy is the key to the solution of most of Man's resource problems; as we have seen, given sufficient energy (together with the technology and industry needed to apply it) food and materials can always be supplied as needed (see Appendix 1 to Chapter 6). Minerals could be extracted from low-grade deposits and water desalinated. Even the area of good farmland need no longer be a limit now that agriculture can, when required, reinforce solar energy with fuel energy.

Apart from human skills, then, the primary requirements are energy, technology and money. Technology to develop such uses of energy; and money to turn the technology into new industries. Indeed, the only ultimate needs are technology and money, for, as we have seen, given these, even energy could be supplied abundantly from, for example, nuclear breeder reactors, nuclear fusion, solar energy, geothermal sources, winds, waves, tides, district heating schemes, and heat pumps. There could however be a fundamental energy limit set by severe climatic changes, if the heat released by our activities grew to about 1% of the daily solar input. We are nevertheless some 100 years away, as yet, from this problem. For the longer future, J. Fremlin (*Be Fruitful and Multiply*, Rupert Hart-Davis, 1972) has vividly described the nightmarish conditions that will develop within 20 generations from now, if Man presses on relentlessly with population growth at the present rate and succeeds in solving all his technical problems except the final one of overheating.

Future World Trends, 1975–2025

Let us consider the next fifty years. In recent decades the Gross World Product (GWP), i.e. the sum of all countries' individual Gross Domestic Products (GDP), has been growing on average at about 5% a year, i.e., doubling every 14 years. On this basis and starting from a 1975 GWP of about $4100 billion, we arrive at the estimates given in the table below, i.e. $14 000 b in the year 2000 and $47 000 b in 2025. Projected world populations are also given in Table 6.1, based on the United Nations' medium estimates (see Fig. 6.1), and from these we deduce the 'average personal incomes', i.e. GWP per person, for the years in question.

Table 6.1   World Economic and Population Projections
(1975 prices)

	1975	2000	2025
World			
Gross World Product (GWP), $billion	4100	14 000	47 000
Population, billion	4	6.1	8.6
GWP per person, $	1025	2300	5500
Developed Countries			
Gross Product (GP), $billion	3450	11 800	39 600
Population, billion	1.1	1.4	1.6
GP per person, $	3140	8430	24 700
Less Developed Countries			
Gross Product, $billion	650	2200	7400
Population, billion	2.9	4.7	7.0
GP per person, $	225	470	1060

All these figures are of course merely projections, into the future, of recent trends. The question to be asked is whether the world's resources will be sufficient to sustain such rates of growth. In considering this, it is important first to break the figures down, as shown in the table, into separate groups for the developed and less developed countries. This brings out the great contrast between the first group, less than a third of the world's peoples, with large personal incomes yet inclined to take their GDP growths mainly as increased personal incomes; and the second group, over 70% of the world's peoples with minute personal incomes yet inclined to take rather more of their GDP growths as increased populations than as increased personal incomes. Questions could of course be asked about the wisdom of these social choices but, purely from the standpoint of environmental economics, what matters is whether the world's natural and economic resources will be able to support such growths.

Before we turn to this, however, it will be convenient to consider Table 6.1 from the standpoint of the economics of population control. We see that the 11-fold increase in the projected Gross Product for the less-developed countries, over the period to 2025, is very largely offset by the projected population growths for those countries, with the result that the projected GP per person grows only 4-fold, to an income only one-third of that already reached now in the developed countries. By

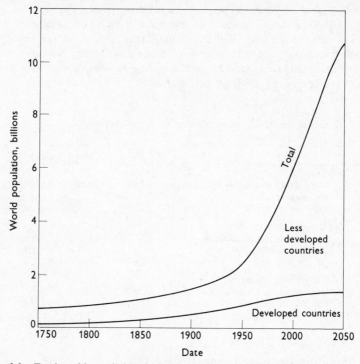

Fig. 6.1   Total world population shown as that for the less developed countries added above that for the developed countries, based on United Nations Data and Medium Estimates.

contrast, if the population in the less-developed countries were to grow by no more than the same factor as that projected for the developed ones, it would reach only about 4.2 billion in 2025, instead of 7.0 b, in which case the GP per person could be $1760, i.e. a 7-fold growth.

This benefit in GP per person would be gained through an approximate halving of the presently projected population growth rate in the less developed countries. The number of births thus prevented would be about 2.8 b, i.e. about equal to the present total population of the less developed countries. The costs of modern contraceptives, i.e. the 'pill', or the intra-uterine devices (IUD), are about $3 to $10 per prevented birth. The total expenditure on population control, for the above result, would thus amount to some $10 b to $30 b, which is very small compared with the projected Gross Product for the less-developed countries. No investment of such sums, in industry or agriculture, could achieve anything like such a large effect as this on the future GP per person in these countries. Hence the widely held view that 'less than five dollars invested in population control is worth a hundred dollars invested in economic growth'.

We shall, nevertheless, assume in the following estimates that the future world population will follow the UN medium projections, as summarized in Table 6.1.

Agriculture

At the present time the developed countries require the equivalent of about $\frac{3}{4}$ ton of grain per person annually, much of it converted into animal products, whereas the less developed countries mostly have to manage on only $\frac{1}{4}$ ton. The world average is thus a little below 0.4 ton per person. Without changing this average, if the developed countries could be content with 0.5 per person, the less developed ones could then have 0.36 per person, and everyone in principle could be well, if not luxuriously fed. On this basis, only a small (although by no means easily accomplished) increase in present food production, suitably distributed, would be needed to *secure* this average for today's population. By contrast, very large increases of grain production will be needed, in proportion with the growth of population, to keep up the same average per person, in future, as Table 6.2 shows.

Table 6.2   World Food Requirements

	1975	2000	2025
Population, billion	4	6.1	8.6
Annual Grain Equivalent, billion tons	1.6	2.4	3.4

These are consumers' requirements. Because of losses between farm and consumer the production figures of grain on the farms, at today's rates of loss, have to be about one-quarter to one-third higher.

Most of this increase will have to be produced on existing farmland, i.e. arable farming will have to become more *intensive*, since there is little unused good land left in those parts of the world where it is needed. Moreover, most of the increased productivity will have to be achieved on the farms of those less developed countries which have the great populations. At the present time these countries have about 740 million hectares of arable land, which yield about 0.9 billion tons a year. This would evidently have to be raised threefold, if the projected requirements for the year 2025 are to be met.

Such a target is extremely severe. Even the developed countries at present achieve a general average of not much more than two tons per hectare at the present time. Nevertheless, there are some hopeful signs. Highly intensive farms in developed countries produce some five tons per hectare.

Moreover, good productivities (three to four tons per hectare) are achieved in several countries such as Japan, Egypt, Taiwan, and Korea on scientifically based labour-intensive small farms, which use a lot of fertilizer and irrigation but only a little machinery. Their small agricultural machines are used, not to replace human labour, but to help individual farmers to grow more by their own personal efforts on one-hectare plots. This is a good model for future agriculture in those less developed countries which have a surplus of manpower and a shortage of capital.

The major inputs — fertilizers, seeds, irrigation, pesticides, weed-killers, capital equipment and fuel — needed to produce these grain outputs in less developed countries could in principle be all provided, given the necessary energy and finance. The biggest claims on energy will be for fertilizers, irrigation, machinery and fuel. According to Pimentel et al. (*Science*, **182**, 2 November 1973, p. 443) the USA in 1970 required the energy of one ton of coal-equivalent per hectare to raise five tons of corn per hectare. Of this energy, about 36% went in fertilizer, nearly 60% in machinery and fuel, and the rest in miscellaneous inputs. Only 1.2% went in irrigation — but only 3.8% of the USA's corn acres are irrigated.

On the small labour-intensive farms of the less developed countries, the machinery and fuel requirements will be relatively small, although not zero because of essential needs for small farm machines, grain stores and transport. On the other hand, far more hectares will need irrigating than in the USA, so that the average irrigation energy costs for intensive general agriculture in those countries might run to about $\frac{1}{4}$ ton coal-equivalent per hectare. Fertilizer needs will also be heavy, amounting in the year 2025 to about $\frac{1}{3}$ ton of coal-equivalent per hectare. Hence the average world requirement for energy, to support its arable farming in 2025, might amount to $\frac{3}{4}$ ton of coal-equivalent per hectare, i.e. about 1200 mtce altogether. This is about 1/7th of the world's present total energy consumption. Could it be provided, for future farming? Clearly the answer is yes, especially when we note that, at present, the amount of energy spent in processing food, *after* it has left the farms, is about twice that actually used on the farms. It must surely be possible, given new technology and some changes in present customs and practices, to make substantial economies in these 'downstream' consumptions of energy on food, sufficient to offset the increased farm requirements.

The financial demands of such a world agricultural programme will be extremely heavy. The World Food Conference in 1974 took note that $5 b a year of foreign exchange was needed immediately by the less developed countries, to increase their food production. Looking further in the future, the costs rise tremendously. Consider for example nitrogen fertilizer. In 1974 it cost $100 m to build a plant to produce 1000 tons daily. The additional fertilizer needed to feed the extra people in 2025, on the basis of the above figures, will be about 700 thousand tons daily. Hence some 700 *additional* nitrogen plants will be needed over the next

50 years at a total (1974) cost of $70 b, or on average at $1.4 b a year. The fuel needed to run them all will amount to about 400 m tons of coal-equivalent a year, at an annual cost of about $10 b at present prices. Irrigation costs could be even higher. Typically, the capital costs of an irrigation system are of order $1000 per hectare, so that on this basis a total of some $900 b might be required for the less developed countries by 2025, i.e. an average of $18 b a year. Another way of judging the size of the financial problem is to recognize that, whereas the peasant farmer in a poor country today can afford to spend each year only about $3 per hectare on his subsistence agriculture, the required threefold increase in productivity might require $100 per hectare annually, for fertilizer, seed, irrigation, and the other essentials of modern, labour-intensive farming. This totals about $90 b a year to be required eventually, i.e. about 2.2% of present GWP.

Materials

Following on Chapter 3, we now look at future trends in the supply and consumption of iron, aluminium and copper. The present annual world demand for these primary products, in millions of tons, is approximately 500 (iron), 14 (aluminium) and 7.5 (copper). The analysis of trends for individual countries (*Materials Requirements in the United States and Abroad in the Year 2000*, University of Pennsylvania, March 1973) shows that, as a country's prosperity grows, a significant change occurs when its GDP per person climbs beyond $2000. Up to this point, the consumption of all materials rises rapidly with increasing personal incomes. Beyond, it, far less of the additional wealth goes into material goods, although the demand for aluminium still continues to increase vigorously, albeit at a lower rate than formerly. In the USA, for example, the amount of steel available per person is now almost steady at ten tons and the annual consumption is unlikely to grow beyond about one ton per person, much of it simply for replacements. Similarly, when the amount of copper available per person reaches about 0.1 tons (at the $2000 income point) the demand thereafter is mainly for replacements. Aluminium, on the contrary, has continued even in the USA to claim an increasing share of the GDP. Summarizing these disparate changes into global average trends, it seems that the overall world demands may grow annually at about 3.5% (iron), 6% (aluminium) and 4% (copper), on which basis the future primary production requirements are estimated as in Table 6.3.

Table 6.3   World Requirements for Primary Metals

	1975	2000	2025
Iron, million tons a year	500	1200	2800
Aluminium, million tons a year	14	60	260
Copper, million tons a year	7.5	20	54

As regards iron we are fortunate, first in that high-grade deposits are available in huge amounts, sufficient to last hundreds of years at present rates of consumption; and second in that less energy is required, per ton of metal, to produce iron than any other common metal. On the basis of present-day practices and figures, the 2800 m tons to be produced in 2025 will require some 2000 mtce, i.e. about one-quarter of present world energy output, and will provide $300 b worth of pig iron. By spending about as much energy again, together with the addition of steel scrap, this iron could become about 4500 m tons of rolled steel, worth about $1400 b.

Bauxite ore is still quite plentiful, but the demand for aluminium is growing so fast that clay may shortly have to become the starting material instead. Clay is a cheap, abundant, resource but its conversion to aluminium may require 25% more energy than bauxite, unless new processes are developed. The main economic constraint in present aluminium production is the very high energy cost, about 7 tce per ton of metal, from mine to ingot. In the USA, for example, over 5% of the total electricity output is now consumed in aluminium production. In terms of present-day practices and figures, the 260 m tons of aluminium to be produced in 2025 will require some 1800 mtce (including the annual coal-equivalent of a half million megawatts of electricity generation) and will provide about $110 b of aluminium ingots.

Copper could be difficult. Already, the grade of ore mined has dropped from about 5% of copper during the last century, to 1% in 1950 and only about 0.6% today. Geological indications are that large deposits exist at about 0.1% copper, but they would be very expensive to extract, e.g. costing about 20 tce and $10 000 per ton of copper produced. At this rate, in terms of present-day practices and figures, the 54 m tons to be produced in 2025 would require some 1000 mtce and cost about $500 b, to provide only some $50 b of copper at today's prices! Clearly, a simple extrapolation of present trends makes no sense in this case and we may expect copper prices to rise greatly, during the next 50 years, and other materials to substitute extensively for the metal.

Plastics and Petrochemicals

Pressure on the world's fossil fuel resources, particularly oil, has been further intensified in recent years through the phenomenal growth of the petrochemical industries, which make plastics, synthetic fibres and other products from petroleum. The use of plastics has increased in some countries by 18% annually, i.e. has doubled every four years. In the USA, for example, the production of plastics has grown from about 0.1 m tons in 1940 to 1 m in 1950 and 10 m in 1970. If such trends continue, the tonnage of plastics will exceed that of steel before the end of the century. It seems doubtful whether such extraordinary growths will be sustained however, partly because when the tonnage approaches that of the bulk constructional materials the opportunities for further great expansions will diminish, but more substantially because of future world shortages of cheap oil. If we assume, rather arbitrarily, that the future world requirements for plastics will increase slightly faster than aluminium, e.g. will grow at 7% a year, the long-term trends are as follows:

World Requirements for Plastics

	1975	2000	2025
Million tons a year	60	325	1800

Plastics are energy-intensive materials. Thus, petroleum products amounting to the equivalent of about three tons of coal are required to produce one ton of plastics. On the basis of present-day practices and figures, the 1800 m tons a year projected for the year 2025 would thus require some 5400 mtce, which is about two-thirds of present world energy output, and they would provide about $2000 b worth of materials.

Energy

By simplifying the world's multifarious food and material needs down to a few major ones, which are dependent upon energy and money, and thereby assuming that all other shortages can be overcome by substitution and new technology, we have taken an optimistic view of the general problem of meeting the world's future needs. Summarizing the above estimates, the projected future world energy requirements for farming and basic materials in round figures are given in Table 6.4.

Table 6.4 World Energy Requirements for Farming and some Basic Materials
(millions of tons of coal-equivalent)

	1975	2000	2025
Farming	400	750	1 200
Steel	700	1 700	4 000
Aluminium	100	450	1 800
Copper	30	150	1 000
Plastics	200	1 000	5 500
Total	1 430	4 050	13 500
Total, per person, tons	0.36	0.67	1.6

This growth, at over 4% a year, is much greater than the projected growth of population, and would carry the required expenditure of energy from about one-sixth of present world energy, now, to nearly twice present world energy, in 2025.

Allowing for the fact that most energy today is used for other purposes, a *lower limit* to the future demand, on the basis of the above projections, is thus obtainable by assuming that the demand for these other purposes stays constant. On this basis, the world demand would grow from about 8500 mtce today to some 12 500 in the year 2000 and 22 000 in 2025, i.e. a growth of about 2.1% a year, which is somewhat faster than the projected population growth rate. In practice, the world's energy consumption has been growing since 1960 at about 5% a year (apart from an interruption after the 1973 oil crisis). On this basis, the demand in mtce might run up to 29 000 in the year 2000 and even to 98 000 in 2025, figures that would easily accommodate those for the energy of food and basic materials. However, future continuing growths at 5% a year seem unrealistically high. They would, for example, given everyone in 2025 the equivalent of over 11 tons of coal annually, on average, which is about as high as present USA consumption and twice that in most other industrial countries. Moreover, it would mean that the proportion of world energy spent on farming and materials would fall considerably between now and 2025, which seems an unrealistic projection of future trends in the light of the estimated strongly increasing energy requirements for these basic human needs. It seems more socially realistic to suppose that total energy requirements will grow rather less rapidly than this. For example, at a growth of 3.5% a year, the world energy consumption would be as follows:

Projected World Total Energy
Requirements
(at 3.5% p.a. Growth Rate)

	1975	2000	2025
Mtce:	8500	20 000	48 000

This would easily cover the requirements for food and basic materials and still leave the greater part for general industrial, commercial, and domestic uses.

But, can it be met? The answer in purely physical terms, as we have seen in Chapter 2, is yes; although it would mean a gigantic development of the world's energy resources, e.g. doubling of oil recovery (at present only about 30% of capacity) from existing oil fields, working of marginal fields, extraction from tar sands and oil shales, expansion of coal industries, use of nuclear breeder reactors, development of alternative new energy sources, and improved energy conservation measures. The amounts could be provided, but the cost will be very high. For instance, even to double the supply of natural oil might necessitate a doubling of its unit price, to over $20 a barrel (see *Important for the Future*, UN Institute for Training and Research, September 1976). Capital costs would also be very large.

Nevertheless, so long as the cost of energy rises gradually, its effect can be accommodated without intolerable strain by a growing economy. For example, if fuel prices were to rise a further $10 a barrel (i.e. by about $50 per ton of coal-equivalent), the costs to be absorbed, on the basis of the above energy projections, would be as follows:

Possible Increased Costs of World Energy (at Constant money value)

	1975	2000	2025
Extra energy cost, $b.	400	1 000	2 400
GWP, $b.	4 100	14 000	47 000

These figures may be compared with the projections for GWP, on the assumption of a continuing growth of 5% a year. We see that the effect at the present time would amount to about 10% of GWP, i.e. equivalent to 2 years' economic growth at this 5% a year rate (which is comparable with the actual time of world economic recession that followed the roughly $10 rise in crude oil prices at the end of 1973). If such an increase were taken a little at a time, over a decade or more, its effect could be absorbed and still leave over 80% of the annual growth of wealth untouched. In later years, the extra cost would itself rise considerably, due to the growth in energy consumption, but on the basis of the above figures this would be more than offset by the growth in GWP, so that its economic effect would be rather less severe.

It is of course doubtful whether the world's economy will grow in future by 5% a year. But even if it becomes only 3.5% a year, so reaching about $23 000 b in the year 2025, the extra energy cost of $2400 b could easily be found, over the 50 year period, by offsetting a minor fraction of each year's additional wealth, e.g. by dropping the *net* growth rate (total growth minus energy offset) of GWP to about 3.3% a year.

Conclusion

We have thus arrived at a possible world scenario for the next fifty years, based on the UN medium estimates of population growth, which average about 1.6% p.a. through to the year 2025, and an assumed growth in Gross World Product (GWP) of 3.5% p.a. at constant money values. Both assumptions represent rather lower growths than in the recent past. In the scenario, enough food is provided to enable everyone to be reasonably well-fed, although not at the luxurious standards now reached in some affluent countries, and other materials and energy are also adequately provided. These provisions could all be made, given adequate forward planning to enable the necessary technology and new industries to be developed ready for when they are needed, although the financial costs would be very high. The extra energy cost would amount to about 10% of GWP by the year 2025. Allowing also 2% for anti-pollution measures, 12% of GWP would thus have to be offset for these purposes. Nevertheless, spread over 50 years, this would average only a reduction of annual GWP growth from its basic value of 3.5% p.a. to a *net disposable* value of slightly over 3.2% p.a. (see Fig. 6.2). This net 3.2% would then, again on average, be half used in increasing the population by 1.6% p.a. and half in raising the world's material standard of living which, at 1.6% p.a., would double in about 44 years. The scenario is summarized in Table 6.5.

Table 6.5   Possible World Scenario, 1975 to 2025
(b = 1 000 000 000)

	1975	2000	2025
Population, b.	4	6.1	8.6
GWP, $b (3.5% p.a. growth)	4 100	9 700	23 000
GWP per person, $	1 025	1 600	2 700
Annual Grain Equivalent, b. tons	1.6	2.4	3.4
Annual Iron, b. tons	0.5	1.2	2.8
Annual Aluminium, m. tons	14	60	260
Annual Copper, m. tons	7.5	20	54
Annual Plastics, m. tons	60	325	1 800
Annual Energy, btce	8.5	20	48
Extra energy cost, $b	–	1 000	2 400
Extra anti-pollution cost, $b	–	200	460
Net disposable GWP, $b	4 100	8 500	20 000
Net GWP per person, $	1 025	1 400	2 300

The problems of achieving such a scenario are environmental, technological, industrial, economic, social and political. As we have seen, the environmental problems of resources and pollution can be solved by the allocation of energy and finance, allowing time for the necessary technological and industrial developments. Energy is the key to most of the material problems but adequate supplies may not be possible except at unit prices well above the present level, as is taken into account in the scenario; but even a future growth rate in GWP of only 3.5% p.a. should be sufficient to accommodate fairly easily the burdens of additional resources and anti-pollution costs, provided that these can be absorbed gradually

The real problems are not environmental and economic, but social and political: whether the rich countries will moderate their appetites for food and wealth; whether the overcrowded poor countries will moderate their appetites for large families; whether the resources necessary to solve the food-growing problems in the overcrowded poor countries will be provided and effectively used; whether the world will make other help available to enable these poor countries to increase their incomes per person above their present desperately low levels; whether all countries will be willing

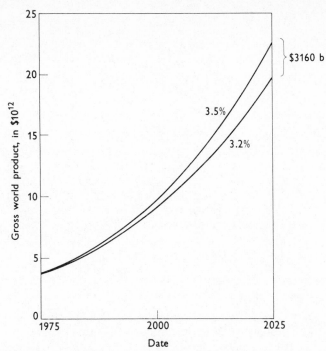

Fig. 6.2 An offset of 12% in GWP, amounting to $2800 billion in the year 2025, for extra energy and pollution costs, could be accommodated within a 0.3% p.a. change in growth rates.

slightly to forego other benefits in order to preserve and improve the quality of their environment; and whether they will take the necessary early actions to ensure that alternative supplies of energy will be sufficiently available before the present supplies are exhausted.

Appendix 1 Input–output Analysis

Detailed information on the flows of materials, energy, manufactures, etc. through a national economy is conveniently expressed through the method of *input–output analysis* (see W. Leontief, *Scientific American*, vol. 212, page 25, 1965; and *Input–Output Economics*, Oxford University Press, 1966). The following table represents a highly simplified *input–output matrix* for an imaginary country whose total economy is divided into just two sectors, i.e. agriculture and industry:

From Sector	To Sector Agriculture	Industry	To Final Consumers	Gross Output
Agriculture	10	20	20	50
Industry	15	85	150	250
Value Added	25	145		

Reading across the table, along the first row, we see that the agricultural sector supplied 10 units (e.g. $b) of its output to itself (e.g. cattle food and seeds), 20 units to the industrial sector (e.g. wheat to bakeries and barley to breweries) and 20 direct to final consumers (e.g. vegetables to market), making a gross output of 50 units from this sector. Reading down the first column we see that the agricultural sector received 10 units of input from itself and 15 from industry (e.g. farm machinery) and generated an *added value* of 25 by its own efforts, so making its gross output of 50. The corresponding figures in the second row and column represent the outputs and inputs of the industrial sector. The supplies to final consumers (20 + 150) and the values added (25 + 145) both sum to the same *net output* or *gross national product* of 170 units.

Actual input–output tables, which divide national economies into dozens of different sectors (e.g. coal mining, mineral oil refining, coke ovens, gas, electricity, as different energy sectors) enable the flows of various resources through the economies to be traced and from them the primary resource inputs into the various final products can be determined, as well as the sensitivity of the outputs to changes in the costs of these inputs. Summary input–output tables for the United Kingdom in 1970, which distinguish 35 different economic sectors, were published in

Economic Trends (Central Statistical Office) in May 1974 (HMSO). The US Department of Commerce publishes an 83-sector table annually. Input—output analysis has been applied to energy problems by Anne Carter (*Science*, vol. 184, page 325, 1974) and recently to future world trends by W. Leontief (*The Future of the World Economy*, Oxford University Press, to be published).

Further Reading

References are listed by chapter and are arranged for progressive reading.

Chapter 1 Earth, Air, Fire and Water

SAMUELSON, P. (1976) *Economics*, McGraw-Hill, Kogakusha
LIPSEY, R. G. (1975) *An Introduction to Positive Economics*, Weidenfeld and Nicholson, London
ROLL, E. (1973) *A History of Economic Thought*, Faber, London
GEORGESCU-ROEGEN, N. (1974) *The Entropy Law and the Economic Process*, Harvard University Press, Cambridge, Mass.
BOULDING, K. E. (1966) 'The Economics of the Coming Spaceship Earth', *Environmental Quality in a Growing Economy*, Jarrett, H., Ed., Johns Hopkins University Press, Baltimore
PEARCE, D. W. (1976) *Environmental Economics*, Longman, London

Chapter 2 Energy

Scientific American (September 1970) 'The Biosphere'
                     (September 1971) 'Energy and Power'
HUBBERT, M. K. (1962) *Energy Resources*, National Academy of Sciences – National Research Council Publication 1000-D, Washington D.C.
CHAPMAN, P. F. (1975) *Fuel's Paradise*, Penguin Books, Harmondsworth
PHILLIPSON, J. (1966) *Ecological Energetics*, Edward Arnold, London
ION, D. C. (1975), *Availability of World Resources*, Graham and Trotman
ENERGY RESEARCH GROUP, CAVENDISH LABORATORY (1976) *Energy Prospects*, Advisory Council on Energy Conservation, HMSO, London
CONNELLY, P. and PERLMAN, R. (1975) *The Politics of Scarcity*, Royal Institute of International Affairs and Oxford University Press
BARNETT, H. J. and MORSE, C. (1963) *Scarcity and Growth*, Johns Hopkins for Resources for the Future, Inc., Baltimore

Chapter 3 Minerals

COMMITTEE ON RESOURCES AND MAN (1969) *Resources and Man*, National Academy of Sciences and National Research Council, San Francisco
SUTULOV, A. (1972) *Minerals in World Affairs*, University of Utah Printing Services, Salt Lake City.

WARREN, K. (1973) *Mineral Resources*, Penguin Books, Harmondsworth
MADDOX, J. (1972) 'Raw Materials and the Price Mechanism', *Nature*, **236**, p. 331, London

Chapter 4 Food

Scientific American (September 1976) 'Food and Agriculture'
BORGSTROM, G. (1967) *The Hungry Planet*, Collier, New York
BROWN, L. R. and ECKHOLM, E. P. (1974) *By Bread Alone*, Praeger Publishers, New York
LEACH, G. (1976) *Energy and Food Production*, IPC Science and Technology Press, Guildford
MELLANBY, K. (1975) *Can Britain Feed Itself?*, The Merlin Press, London
EHRLICH, P. R. and ERLICH, A. H. (1970) *Population, Resources, Environment*, W. H. Freeman, Reading
SOLOMON, M. E. (1976) *Population Dynamics*, Edward Arnold, London
TAYLOR, L. R., Ed. (1970) *The Optimum Population for Britain*, Academic Press, London

Chapter 5 The Natural Environment

STUDY OF CRITICAL ENVIRONMENTAL PROBLEMS (SCEP) (1970) *Man's Impact on the Global Environment*, M.I.T. Press, Cambridge, Mass.
WARD, B. and DUBOS, R. (1972) *Only One Earth*, Penguin Books, Harmondsworth
ROYAL COMMISSION ON ENVIRONMENTAL POLLUTION (1972) *Third Report*, HMSO Cmnd. 5054, London
BECKERMAN, W. (1975) 'Pricing for Pollution', *Hobart Paper 66*, The Institute of Economic Affairs, London
VICTOR, P. A. (1972) *Economics of Pollution*, Macmillan, London
US GOVERNMENT PRINTING OFFICE (1972) 'The Economic Impact of Pollution Control', *Report No* 1972-0-458-471, Washington D.C.
MELLANBY, K. (1972) *The Biology of Pollution*, Edward Arnold, London

Chapter 6 The Next Fifty Years

BROWN, H., Ed. (1967) *The Next Ninety Years*, California Institute of Technology
FREMLIN, J. H. (1972) *Be Fruitful and Multiply*, Rupert Hart-Davies, London
OHLIN, G. (1967) *Population Control and Economic Development*, OECD, Paris
FORRESTER, J. (1971) *World Dynamics*, Wright-Allen Press
GOLDSMITH, E. R. D. et. al., Eds. (1972) 'A Blueprint for Survival', *The Ecologist*, **2**, p. 2, London

MEADOWS, D. H. et. al. (1972) *The Limits to Growth*, Universe Books, New York and Earth Island, London

MESAROVIC, M. and PESTEL, E. (1975) *Mankind at the Turning Point*, Hutchinson, London

COLE, H. S. D. et. al., Eds. (1973) *Thinking about the Future*, Chatto and Windus for Sussex University Press

MADDOX, J. (1972) *The Doomsday Syndrome*, Macmillan, London

LEONTIEF, W. W. (1966) *Input–Output Economics*, Oxford University Press

CARTER, A. P. (1974) 'Applications of Input–Output Analysis to Energy Problems', *Science*, **184**, p. 325

LEONTIEF, W. W., CARTER, A. P., and PETRI, P. (1977, in press) *The Future of the World Economy*, Oxford University Press

Index